A THOUGHTFUL GUIDE TO
SCIENCE &
RELIGION

USING SCIENCE, EXPERIENCE AND RELIGION
TO DISCOVER YOUR OWN DESTINY

DR MICHAEL MEREDITH

BOOKS

WINCHESTER UK
NEW YORK USA

Copyright © 2005 O Books
O Books is an imprint of John Hunt Publishing Ltd., The Bothy, Deershot
Lodge, Park Lane, Ropley, Hants, SO24 0BE, UK
office@johnhunt-publishing.com
www.O-books.net

Distribution in:
UK
Orca Book Services
orders@orcabookservices.co.uk
Tel: 01202 665432 Fax: 01202 666219 Int. code (44)

USA and Canada
NBN
custserv@nbnbooks.com
Tel: 1 800 462 6420 Fax: 1 800 338 4550

Australia
Brumby Books
sales@brumbybooks.com
Tel: 61 3 9761 5535 Fax: 61 3 9761 7095

New Zealand
Peaceful Living
books@peaceful-living.co.nz
Tel: 64 7 57 18105 Fax: 64 7 57 18513

Singapore
STP
davidbuckland@tlp.com.sg
Tel: 65 6276 Fax: 65 6276 7119

South Africa
Alternative Books
altbook@global.co.za
Tel: 27 011 792 7730 Fax: 27 011 972 7787

Text: © 2005 Michael Meredith

Design: BookDesign™, London

ISBN 1 905047 16 9

A CIP catalogue record for this book is available from the British Library.

Printed in the USA by Maple-Vail Manufacturing Group

The never-ending years roll by
Until the Self of life dawns
and we truly begin to shape our destiny.

FOREWORD

As in his earlier book, Michael Meredith brings together things that many writers allow to drift apart. The absolute necessity of thinking of the life of the mind and the life of the spirit together is deeply rooted in all he writes. Scientific rigour, the exploratory principles of modern intellectual life, all this is inseparable from the study of how humans grow into consciousness of themselves and their world and its divine context.

This is a programme for human maturity – a maturity attained not by technical and conceptual slickness, not by a sacrifice of the intellect in the name of faith, but by an integrated and carefully worked out vision of what full awareness or mindfulness means. We move through intellectual enquiry and scientific analysis into compassion and the vision of God.

Personal and concrete without being just anecdotal, full of solid and demanding argument without being dry, this is a very special book, a 'Grammar of Assent' (to borrow the title of Newman's great work) for a scientific age.

Rowan Williams, Archbishop of Canterbury

"Invoked or not invoked, God is present".

CARL JUNG

C O N T E N T S

FOREWORD
Rowan Williams,, Archbishop of Canterbury

INTRODUCTION

PART I - SCIENCE

PART II - EXPERIENCE

PART III - RELIGION

INTRODUCTION

I was blessed to be born in a railway town where endless streams of laden trucks squealed self-consciously down gradients of 1 in 150, and powdery black smuts exasperated my mother as they polka-dotted her clean white sheets billowing down the long garden line. Blessed because our little terraced house was on the lower slopes of a South Wales hillside, so that I grew up poor in material wealth, but rich in freedom.

My quest to find a deeper meaning of life probably started then, when the contrasts of unspoilt countryside and industrial grime reflected my own joys and suffering. I recollect, early on in my life, wondering if everything had arrived in its present state by accident, or whether it had all been carefully arranged in an underlying order, divinely inspired by an all-knowing God.

As I grew older I felt that science told me all about the patterns of the universe. Today, for example, through an understanding of the physical laws, many complex structures are being unraveled which could eventually lead to humanity creating life itself from simple chemical elements, without recourse to any "living" thing whatsoever.

But even if we do eventually create life itself, science doesn't help us to understand so many things. Why should we feel excitement at the mere thought of creating life? Why does science uncover "beautiful" patterns? Why do we appreciate such things? Why should anything exist in the first place? Even more to the point, can science explain that mystical, unified entity that each of us is, that irreducible me that cannot be replaced, for to me, there is no other! Can science explain the way that we, as individuals, as Self, relate to the whole of existence?

Maybe we are just complex matter. And when others speak of their religious experiences it's just the oxygen-rich environment of their brain over-exciting the electro-magnetic fields of their neurotransmitters. Or maybe we should be open to the possibility of the existence of greater things beyond the physical. Maybe we can even become voyagers who leave behind much of the baggage of life - ego, pride and PhDs - to embrace the mystery of our own personal existence. This book illustrates experiences that may unfold to you, as they have to me, a path where science, experience and religion converge to make known our true destiny.

My journey has taken me beyond the limits of scientific thought. I have heard of, and encountered in my professional and private life, many events, experiences and understandings more awesome than beauty itself, that will never be encompassed by the confines of science. Theories and hypotheses that scientists put forward for the evolution of the cosmos, the solar system and life are not to be confused with absolute truth. Such theories and hypotheses, exciting as they are, can only ever be intelligent, but limited guesses, founded upon secondary observational evidence made in our present day. No one can carry out a definitive experiment, for no one can actually go back to the beginning of time to demonstrate how it all began.

But religion can also be limiting, as I discovered when my journey took me behind the tantalizing veils of world scriptures, into the lives of people who are dedicated to a particular faith, and into sacred places where I have practiced many forms of prayer and meditation. In searching for truth I have found that I have had to beware of time-honored practices, which are often based upon concepts of a fertile imagination and likely to be false or even irrelevant. Then there are philosophies, such as "destructive normality", which implies that human suffering is the normal state of affairs. Such philosophies are basic to some of our cultural and religious traditions, but are they a true reflection of our human condition?

Much of the early revelations and ethics to be found in traditional religious beliefs are, like scientific theories, often overtaken by fresh evidence gathered in today's fast-moving world. Even so, at the very heart of scientific knowledge and religious tradition is the pearl of truth. That pearl is our ultimate goal.

This is my personal journey in search of answers to the mystery of human destiny. I invite you to take the adventure with me. Along the way we will discuss many of the paradoxes of life; meet people with stories to tell as we travel from stardust into many lands, to dream new dreams of cooperation not conflict, intelligence not blindness, motivation and synchronicity not chance alone; to brush against science, uniqueness and our interconnected universe; to set our consciousness against the eternal puzzle of *self* and *being*; to wander into everyday joys and suffering, and to dip our toes into meditation and prayer.

Early on, the book challenges the predominant evolutionary theory and argues that although "selection of the fittest" is involved, the overarching characteristics that drive evolution forward are based upon innate intelligence, motivation and cooperation.

We journey through the incredible human mind; a mind that gives each of us the ability to think logically and so use scientific method to probe our Universe; a mind that allows us to experience emotionally great art and profound music; and most importantly, a mind that contains consciousness, which opens us to a form of transcendence that can become Grace-filled.

By exploring some of the most ancient methods uncovered by religious teaching and investigating meditative prayers, we find a path that guides us towards our ultimate destiny.

The exhilaration of reaching the summit of a mountain is only realized by fully involving our own physical and mental efforts, not by hitching a ride in a helicopter. Similarly there is no way of uncovering the deeper meaning of life by rushing to the last chapter of the book, for our ultimate destiny is only found by taking part in the complete journey.

During our journey we will encounter God many times. I find using the title "God" rather arrogant on my part; for who am I to presume to name something which allowed me to exist, and is responsible for my very *being*? Countless millions of people refer to their Creator by a different name such as: Father, Brahman, Waheguru, Christ, Mother, Lord, Allah, Mother Earth, Jesus, Krishna, Yahweh, Ahura Mazda, Benevolent Ultimate Reality, Greater Consciousness, the Real and so on, and so on. Unfortunately, all of these names have been given a whole range of meanings; meanings which can even justify us killing our fellow travelers on this little planet.

Whatever name we use for our Personal Creator we are going to offend someone. However, I'm not convinced our Personal Creator will really mind what name we use.

I remember my grandmother, or Gran as my sister Joan and I used to call her. She lived in Hereford some three miles walk and twenty-seven train miles away from our home in South Wales. When I was about five years old my cousins were at Gran's and were calling her by a different name, "Nana" I believe. It was like a hammer blow to me, my cherished lady being abused by this alien name! However, she did not mind, only we children minded. Similarly I believe that God will not mind what name we choose to use, only the way in which we use it.

As all spiritual, religious and transcendental journeys are in the final analysis, individual and personal, I strongly recommend that as we journey together you reflect on your own life experiences. I can only tell my story, and point to the existence of gems beyond everyday imagination for you to discover for yourself.

Like all enjoyable journeys it is good to pause now and again as you travel, and wait quietly, "You will then understand what is right and just and keep only to the good man's path, for wisdom will sink into your mind, and knowledge will be your heart's delight. Discretion will keep watch over you, understanding will guard you" (*Proverbs* 2: 9-11).

I hope that you enjoy this journey through science, experience and religion as I have, and that you, like me, will be blessed to come face to face with our human destiny and the underlying purpose of your own life.

PART I

SCIENCE

CHAPTER I

THE LAND OF STARDUST

THE MAZE

AS A TEENAGER I believed that William E Henley had discovered the secret to life when he wrote, "I am the master of my fate: I am the captain of my soul". But now, I'm not so sure. Sometimes I feel more like a mindless grain of sand, rocking back and forth at the bottom of a restless sea, making pointless marks in a world of sedimentary mud. A world that is a speck of meaningless dust in a hundred billion stars of a spiral galaxy. A galaxy that is nothing more than a dying sparkle in a universe of a hundred thousand million galaxies.

Are we merely travelers in an unintelligent universe of twists and turns that simply ends in nothing, in absolutely nothing just our complete and utter death?

Although I have some sympathy for concepts that point to life being a meaningless journey through a chaotic maze of morals, ethics and "spin", I sense much more. More than the explanations offered by science and much that is associated with our world religions. There is a greater meaning even beyond such things as desire, beauty, joy, evil and suffering.

When I was a young man I rushed headlong into the complex maze of life. Several decades of love, marriage, family, homes, and a professional career flashed past, before it dawned on me that although the maze had many pleasures and rewards, it was not deeply satisfying. I became more and more aware that the self-perpetuating universe would inevitably ignore me. I knew that I would never affect the ultimate destiny of the maze itself. It would simply re-form to assume a shape determined by its own holistic reality. Whatever I thought, whatever I said, whatever I did or whatever I achieved would be as nothing in the eons to come. And I realized that all my private life and seemingly important professional achievements were like playing in the shallow waves on the shore of possibilities.

I knew there had to be more. Everything I experienced seemed to be part of the chain of cause and effect. All had purpose. So why, then, did I exist and what was my purpose? Why did the maze exist? What was *its* purpose? Was it all just a game or was the secret of my ultimate purpose to be found within the maze itself?

On sleepless nights I longed to know the answers to these age-old questions. After fifty years experience and at the height of a professional career, I simply gave up. I walked out. Unknown to me I had embarked upon what was to be the most spectacular journey of my life. This book sets out to tell of that journey. Before the giant jigsaw of life came together I found that I had to examine, in some detail, many things, from quantum mechanics to a baby's smile. It has been, for me, a walk through the maze of life into a new dawn of understanding.

At first I had no idea what my journey was about. How could I prepare when I did not know where my life was going? I didn't know what questions to ask. There was no *Lonely Planet* guidebook. But my children were grown and independent, my wife, Jeanette was, as always, tolerant, understanding and helpful.

But set out I did, I broke free from the struggle to perfect, to accumulate. I simply let the world flow past me.

I spent the following years in quiet contemplation, exchanging the hectic life of *doing* to the tranquility of *being*. Slowly my focus changed so that I became convinced that all human life had a deep and significant meaning. I began to search for that meaning and the purpose of my own existence.

Early on in my search I came face to face with a flood of alien ideas, " ... Whoever therefore wants to be a friend of the world makes himself an enemy of God" (*James* 4:4b). It took me many years before such strange thoughts, and other people's suffering, became reconciled with my love of nature and with my belief in a caring God. I came to realize that I was still the same *me* that first looked out at this mesmerizingly beautiful world. The uniqueness of my own existence, my very *being*, blossomed fully into my understanding, until finally, through science, experience and faith I came face to face with my ultimate destiny.

The journey began with much contemplation, which developed to become meditation and prayer. And as my mind opened I became aware of many things. First then, to look at the journey that we have all made as part of the continuum of life, right from the very beginning of it all.

THE JOURNEY TO LIFE

IT WAS ONCE thought that building a complex organism, like a human, was just like creating an intricate sculpture. Today science has shown us that there is vastly more complexity and harmony required. So, the first question I asked myself was, "Just how did all this complexity of life actually start?"

Did our ancestors immediately appear, fully formed, from the twinkle in God's eye, or have we all been led on a merry chase through the last fifteen billion years or so?

Since I believe that God's messages are to be found in ancient world scriptures, such as the Bible's creation myth, the first proposition is very appealing. However, as a scientist, I find the second proposition rational and quite compelling. I could, of course take the easy way out and declare one idea correct and the other false.

Many people today are convinced that there is overwhelming proof for the evolutionary model of the origin of life. Some go on to say that evolution unequivocally verifies that God, afterlife and purpose do not exist. While others with equal vigor, say that the evolutionary story is based upon biased interpretations of scant, and even false evidence, and that ultimate truth is only to be found through scripture and revelation. Such beliefs are but two of a huge spectrum of possibilities.

Evolution from stardust to multi-cellular life forms and

animals is a great theory that helps us to progress our ideas and understanding of the universe in which we find ourselves. As Robin Dunbar in his book *The Trouble with Science* tell us that without a framework theory, we cannot ask questions or design experiments.

First, then I would like you to wander with me a little way into the Garden of Eden as proposed by science.

It turns out to be quite simple:

In the beginning, some fifteen billion years ago, there was a Big Bang. Later masses came together, complex molecules formed; suns and planets coalesced within a hundred billion galaxies. Three and a half billion years ago earth conditions allowed complex molecules to become even more complex, forming such things as proteins, which then went on to become single-cell, bacteria-like, life. Around one billion years ago a massive seismographic shift occurred and cells with a control centre, a nucleus, appeared. The great diversity of life began; all competing and destroying other life forms in a terrifying struggle to survive.

But was it quite that simple?

Many theories to do with the creation of the universe have become common currency today. They include the Big Bang, the universe's background noise, black holes, dark matter, dark energy, red-shift measurements and many more. But when each theory is looked at carefully we find that they are only human ideas, *theories*, not facts. They are often in the form of circular arguments, which after some suitable mathematics and wishful thinking, become accepted as factual.

Typically, we start with: "Scientists have today measured some very low level electromagnetic radiation, a form of 'noise', which seems to be radiating from all parts of the universe." Now it is commonly believed that the Big Bang (if it existed) would have created such "noise" which should still be a faint whisper echoing around the universe. So it is then assumed that the low-level electromagnetic "noise" must have been from the Big Bang, and popular press reports go on to make emphatic statements such as, "By measuring the background noise of the universe we have proved that the Big Bang actually occurred." And this despite the fact that the Big Bang model limits the possible amount of normal matter to a maximum of six percent of the total mass of the universe, and the other ninety four per cent has not yet been detected! Such lack of evidence would suggest to most statisticians that the Big Bang theory is a very long way from being a proven fact.

However, the media takes up this logic spin as a true state of the universe! In reality background noise could be many things including something analogous to ripples on a pond, which again could be caused by many things, and all too often we are inclined to choose our emotional favorites as being the truth.

There is still no direct evidence for many of cosmological theories that are commonly taken as proven. For example, even though the German astronomer, Karl Schwarzschild solved the equations for Einstein's theoretical black holes, way back, in the 1914-18 European War, cosmologists are still searching for collaborating proof of their existence. Perhaps the newer ideas such as gravitational lenses, gravastars, WIMPs (Weakly Interacting Massive Particles), MONDs (Modified Newtonian Dynamics), and the like, may soon eliminate our theoretical dependence on such as the Big Bang anyway!

One of the more recent ideas that I find quite intriguing, puts forward the concept that our universe is one bubble among an infinite number of membranous bubbles which ripple as they wobble through an eleventh dimension; making our universe the result of the collision of two such massive membranes, or "branes". But bubbles, far from presenting us with a solution, simply add one more level of complexity to the already mind-blowing dimensions of reality.

Great theories of the cosmos are the result of outstanding innovative minds. It is amazing that, in time, even these could prove to be no more a true reflection of the real universe than the suggestion that gargoyles on old churches depict the physical manifestations of evil. Yet great theories are an essential part of our journey to ultimate truth.

Theorizing can be self-sustaining, each theory heralding a further set of theories. As one amazing cosmological theory leaps over another, we could well be adding to our knowledge of the universe. However, such a never-ending chain of events falls far short of giving us the clues we need in order to uncover the underlying meaning of our lives. They do not point to our ultimate destiny.

I am fast coming to the conclusion that the cosmological start for the journey to life will always be in the realms of theory. The atoms which make up my physical body may well have started as stardust, so that in one sense the material journey to life could well have started in the stars. But these theories are far removed from any direct evidence, nothing like the repeatable proof required when I was designing airplane simulators, radar equipment and computer peripherals.

Sadly then, theories such as the Big Bang are not necessarily factual, but more an exciting and elaborate belief system.

So what happened next?

Evidence found in sedimentary rocks contains what appear to be fossil stromatolites formed by bacteria, suggesting that reproducing life, an advanced autocatalytic system, in the form of single-cell bacteria, commenced on earth around three and a half billion years ago. Even this simplest life form is much more complex than the recent laboratory experiments of complementary templating mechanisms, where families of cooperating RNA (ribonucleic acids) catalysts direct the synthesis of polypeptides (proteins). This complementary temlating could be likened to producing countless pictures from one negative. Mainstream theory, having assumed that complementary templating "naturally" occurs, goes on to presume that the evolution of this initial life form was aided by the fact that some proteins had been synthesized previously and were contained in a conveniently pre-made bag, constructed from an amphipathic membrane (a membrane made up of two distinct layers of different substances, such as oil and water that under the right conditions may become a bubble.

Lynn Margulis in her book *The Symbiotic Planet* points out that even the most basic life forms consist of a tiny membrane-bounded sphere requiring more than fifteen kinds of DNA (deoxyribonucleic acids) and RNA and nearly five hundred different kinds of protein. It seems then, that this 'simplest' form of life could well be far more sophisticated than a modern city, moreover a completely self-sufficient city, with the ability to reproduce itself in its entirety!

The more one studies, the more it becomes obvious that the best minds in science are struggling to explain just how such a complex set of non-intelligent, sequential, chemically based interactions could have evolved to produce that first life form, especially when it is realized that many metabolic reactions take place together, apparently synchronistically. The relevant literature is filled with "ifs", "maybes", and "possibilities", and proposes that there must have been a "strong evolutionary pressure". Ideas are rife such as those of the Swedish chemist Arrhenius who around a hundred years ago suggested that all terrestrial life was carried to Earth from another region of the Galaxy by particles of cosmic material such as meteorites.

Such ideas, if proved to be true, suggest the availability of a few billion more years for evolution to have started elsewhere in the universe. But even this extra time makes the possibility of life starting by pure chance virtually the same, estimated by some as an impossible $10^{40,000}$ to 1 against! The underlying assumption that there is no intelligent input in the evolutionary process, that all is devoid of cooperation or intrinsic altruistic tendencies, may turn out to be the problem. Could it be that evolutionary procedure may not be as blind as some would have us believe?

Many variations on the single-celled life form existed and dominated the earth for two and a half billion years. Then a mere one billion years ago some cells began to split themselves into two. After splitting some remained together living harmoniously as one life form. This is a strange fact when we realize just how successful simple-cell life forms were and still are. Even today they make up over half the complete biomass of the earth.

So what was it that made one of these single-cell life forms decide to become two cells? What produced the first multi-celled organism and so heralded the amazing complexity of life on Earth as we know it? There is no more perfect a shape than a sphere. A sphere gives minimum surface area to volume ratio, enabling it to interact most effectively with its surroundings. One cell can quite easily, and often does, take up a spherical form; there seems to be no obvious reason why a spherical, reproducing life form should not be the complete story of life. Why split in two and lose some of this advantage?

According to Darwin's theory all adaptations that endure are based upon the new life form having survival advantages over its predecessor. One cell, by becoming two "identical" half-sized cells, will only be able to "eat" smaller packets of food and also be more vulnerable to be eaten itself. The chances of survival for each individual cell appear to have been reduced rather than enhanced. To survive, the new cells would have had to have had some instantaneous advantages over their original form. Perhaps each new cell somehow complemented its twin by being specially suited for a particular task? In which case it seems logical that the two cells would have needed to communicate to each other from the onset, which adds to the complexity required to launch this twin-celled enterprise!

From the evidence of cell division we have today, it seems to me, the first cell that successfully split into two would have produced, in effect, identical twins; each cell being as perfect as the other. How then did the much acclaimed "survival of the fittest" mechanism work here, to make one cell dominant over the other? How did they "decide" who was the top dog, the team leader?

On top of all this the greatest obstacle to overcome in cell reproduction would have been when reproduction changes from asexual to become sexual. This is quite mind-boggling. The change, or mutation, from one cell with both strands of the DNA code intertwined, would require production of a cell containing only half the DNA code, looking for a second cell similarly modified. Complexity would have had to take a giant step *backwards* to produce only one, independent, living DNA strand.

As well as the complex sequences above, one of the cells primed for sexual reproduction, the female, would have to resemble a sophisticated factory with all the process, materials, computing ability and machine tools to synthesize a completely new unique individual cellular life form. It would have to contain numerous extra materials, such as unused proteins, and have the ability to produce thousands of other sub-assemblies, on demand. This "female" cell would then have to seductively loiter in a suitable place to receive complementary DNA instructions from a "male" cell. She even had to be able to distinguish genuine DNA from the millions of imitators that kept knocking on her cell wall. Finally this cell factory would need a very advanced assembly schedule to ensure that events progressed effectively to form new cells.

Meanwhile the other half of the DNA in the simplest of cells, the male, had to have some inbuilt motivation to seek out the female cell, and the ability to find and penetrate its cell wall.

Although countless theories have been put forward for sexual reproduction, such as, it purges the genome of deleterious mutations, none have been successfully verified by rigorous control experiments in the form of a fully acceptable scientific trial. The puzzle remains. A-sexual reproduction, in many respects, appears to be much more effective than sexual reproduction.

Despite our lack of information on how or why the first cell successfully split and asexual to sexual reproduction occurred, split and copulate they did! And a great deal of cooperation, as well as "blind" aggression, must have been involved.

We are told by the professionals, who have analyzed the fossil evidence, that after this amazing reproduction process, cells soon developed high quality communication between them, and also became much more specialized. This has resulted in an estimated thirty million living species today. In just one of these species, Homo sapiens, there are a hundred million million communicating cells, working in unison in each human body. How each cell knows just what organ or function it has to become, or how mere molecules inside our bodies constantly enact their own version of a colossal worldwide telephone system, are two more mysteries that may never be fully uncovered by science alone.

As evolution develops, synergies occur where reinforcements give far more profound results than the simple combination of all the previous individual events and conditions. These synergies become manifest as new and greater levels of cooperating complexity. It is not aggression or conflict - but harmonious communication and what I call, "synchronistic cooperation", coming together, giving rise to the synergy, that allows evolution to jump to a higher level of complexity. Energies bind in each succeeding level of complexity and a form of overarching control appears. It seems then that successive evolutionary changes have resulted in you and me having a consciousness far removed from the atoms and cells that make up our bodies.

Why matter has inbuilt characteristics, compelling it to build itself into more and more complexity, is yet another mystery. I can accept that matter has a range of mechanical and other properties. For example, atoms have either "left" or "right" spin, and display differing electromagnetic features. I do not however, find it logical when it is suggested that these features are the *reason* that atoms become complex. It is a little like saying the reason, or driving force, for reproduction is our possession of sexual organs.

Recent brain research points to our desire being a mental state, controlled by some overall function rather than through local activity or adaptation.

In fact each stage of complexity from the sub-atomic to sophisticated life forms reminds me of my early experience as an apprentice for the Ministry of Aviation in the UK nearly half a century ago. I was taken to the *M O Valve Company* at Hammersmith London, to learn about the automatic assembly of thermionic valves (amplifying devices that predated transistors and microchips) used for early missile systems. To my surprise I was shown several large vibrating and rotating machines in which had been placed intricate pre-formed metal shapes. The little shapes, each in their respective agitating machines, were miniature grids, anodes and cathodes, each about a centimeter long. The amazing movements of these little components fascinated me. They were seemingly alive, jumping and vibrating while slowly rotating in their joyful, chaotic dance. I watched, spellbound, as each component in its turn, as if by magic, orientated and serialized itself precisely with its neighbors while moving around its great shaking universe. Each component then moved on to become perfectly synchronized with its future companions from other machines before being permanently fixed next to them in rapidly solidifying glass pellets. In other words, the system had been conceived and engineered so that chaos and randomness was the vehicle for arranging these simple pre-designed parts so that they "self-assembled" into complex structures.

It was several decades before it occurred to me that the process used during the assembly of those thermionic valves had, to some extent, copied the process of evolution. For evolution is a process where seemingly random chance produces order out of chaos. Over the interceding years I had been interested in the process of evolution and had not been able to reconcile the fact that life became more and more complex, increasing its entropy, while the laws of physics suggest the opposite. I had become, like many before me, mesmerized by the competing agitation in nature and had fallen for the idea that competition "survival of the fittest" was the complete driving force for evolution to occur. I had become so overawed by the dance of established life forms that I had ignored the fact that nature settles down of its own accord and "'piece parts" start to cooperate to form more complex structures.

I concluded that the survival of the fittest may well be part of the micro process of evolution, but the more dominant, macro process was associated with order and cooperation!

In other words the base characteristic, the very process, of cosmological and biological evolution contains both random "aggression" and "cooperating" order; without both of these characteristics our universe would not exist.

Such thoughts led me to question other basic assumptions of science such as the possibility that at the subatomic level, there may be motivational forces at work! Hence, one of the many unanswered questions for science is, "How far down the tree of life does internal motivation apply, is it in fact intrinsic to all matter and energy forms?" Science has not even begun to consider, let alone possess any equipment sensitive enough to measure, the possible motivation that may be within simple matter. In fact science has only observed motivation/desire in living things, and even then in only a very limited way.

Does evolutionary theory prove that there is no guiding influence behind the process itself? Does it eliminate God? No, it does neither of these things. In fact, if we use our own knowledge and experience of life, we *know* that motivation is inbuilt. Children do not learn to crawl by being taught arm and leg movements. Motivation is derived from an inner urge to move towards some goal.

Is there then, an unsolved conundrum right at the outset of our understanding matter itself, and how it becomes complex? Before coming to our conclusion we must explore a little more of our world that has caused great minds such as Alfred Wallace and Charles Darwin to infer that we are all only part of a blind evolutionary process.

THE EVOLVED ANIMAL

THE BIG BANG is a belief system, which cannot be definitively proved. How life began is equally uncertain. The division into multi-cellular forms has many irrationalities and is yet another problem to try to explain logically. Maybe cooperation and motivation are more important than randomness and aggression in the story of evolution. Let's look at the natural world for a moment, openly and rationally, and try to ascertain how complexity may have arisen from relative simplicity.

A question that has intrigued me for much of my life has been, "Are we as human beings, simply specialized animals?" Although our DNA is within a few percentage points of many animal life forms there seems to be no clear answers. Hindus, Buddhists, American Indians, and Darwinians, see no problem with us being part of the spectrum of animal life. Jews, Christians and Muslims refer to their common religious scripture that tells them that God made man instantaneously from the clay of the earth, and that unlike animals, we are made in God's image. Despites all our differences I am sure that we can at least agree that we share some of the animal kingdom's physical characteristics, such as movement, digestion, breeding and sleeping.

There is much debate about the details of the dominant evolutionary theory that is believed to have produced the diversity of life on earth today. For example, did humans evolve from a type of

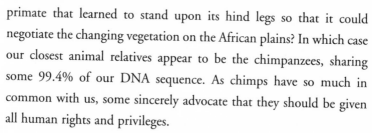

primate that learned to stand upon its hind legs so that it could negotiate the changing vegetation on the African plains? In which case our closest animal relatives appear to be the chimpanzees, sharing some 99.4% of our DNA sequence. As chimps have so much in common with us, some sincerely advocate that they should be given all human rights and privileges.

However, other studies conclude that our evolution is from an altogether different evolutionary branch. Nakedness, sweating, tears, and even the organs of speech are much nearer to water–loving mammals such as the hippopotamus and sea lion, than they are to the primate. In fact it is hard to imagine how such things as our larynx for speech, could have evolved without our ancestors needing to control their breathing, perhaps through adapting to interact with deep water, at some time or other. Monkeys cannot even hold their breath; human babies can swim at birth.

The remnant tail at the base of our spines, the webbed hands and feet of early developing human fetuses and the fact that much of the same DNA sequence can be found in both earthworms and humans, all point to some form of *evolutionary process* which has made our bodies the shape that they are today. It is therefore understandable that many interpret the bond between all life forms as stemming from a common ancestor. And they could well be right.

Darwin's great work, which tells us so much, nevertheless may not be the complete story of how the plant and animal kingdoms came to be. As first-hand experience is the best, I wanted to experience some observations of my own and discover for myself any overall pattern that may be common to both man and beast. Using the incentive of a week relaxing on an African beach I managed to persuade my wife, Jeanette, to leave her Cognitive Behavioral Therapy practice for a few weeks. And so we set off to explore some of the most natural game reserves in the world, the East African game parks of Kenya and Tanzania.

The following few paragraphs *from my log* give a snap shot of what we observed:

On the *Endless Plain* of the Serengeti there were millions of contented wildebeest in huge breeding herds, spread out over the vastness, telescoping away to become like swarms of small, black insects which disappeared over the curvature of the earth.

The thirty million-year old Great Rift Valley includes one of the largest calderas in the world, the Ngorongoro Crater. Seven thousand foot peaks join together to make a twenty-kilometer diameter crater rim. Within the crater some of our great land mammals and birds live out their natural life span:

Relaxed wildebeest wander freely from protective birth groups to spread out and polka dot the greenery.

A small group of zebras contentedly graze across the lower slopes; striped "humbugs" coalescing to make one graceful *Swan Lake* ballerina in their mesmerizing, ever-changing patterns of black and white.

In open meadowlands the solitary eland roam with the multitude, the hartebeest, impala, gazelles, warthog, crown cranes, bustards and more. Ostrich stride purposefully about, while fox-like jackals run the gauntlet through it all. In the centre of the multitude some half a kilometer away, I saw young hyena cubs tumbling about with pleasure in the warming sun. But I was not the only one to see them, for a line of rippling muscle walked through the lounging crowds towards them. As danger neared, the cubs scampered below; the adults ran, stopped and half turned to smile and stare out the, now stationary, foot-stamping challenge of four great African buffalo.

A massive lone tusker dominated, and then walked to become an insignificant dot in a world of balance.

A family of hippos, each animal over a tonne, played and polluted the pools while spoonbills swung their beaks back and forth to find satisfaction within the murky salt-pool stench. Pink carpets of flamingos rippled with contentment.

A pride of lions flopped in luxurious helplessness, legs outstretched to sacrifice their limp paws to the hot sun.

What then can I conclude from such an experience? All seemed to be at peace and harmony with gentle protective mothering love. And yet in all this beauty and tranquility, death was perilously close. The venomous fangs of a green mamba snake are capable of killing a man in fifteen minutes. A lion can suffocate its prey in less. However, the great majority of carcasses on the great African plains are of the very young, the weak and the old; and this is true for game and carnivore alike. Animals of all kinds when in their prime move alertly, like a city walker in the early hours of morning. They know their patch. There are always accidents. Death can come to anyone, but it is relatively rare for animals in their prime.

The survival of the fittest between species is not the overriding characteristic on the great plains of Africa, although there are fights between adults of the same species when food is scarce, or when the inner, maddening urge to breed strikes the males. Aggression between experienced, fit adults of different species is much less common. We saw lions kill the vulnerable, but stand silent when faced with the sharp horns and bone-shattering hooves of a wildebeest in its prime. The carnivores reminded me of school bullies as they sought out the weak, usually at night.

And then I knew that although Darwin's selection of the fittest theory appears to be at play in the natural world, it is only part of the picture. The main driving force that I observed was more the power of surging individualism and the impact of cooperating collectiveness, apparently derived from the internal motivation within each beast.

Then again, if survival of the fittest were the dominant parameter between species, surely after billions of years things would have evolved into a stable monoculture fully adapted to climate changes? Yet, when I walk down a county road in a Welsh springtime and see the luxuriance of the hedgerows, there is not a dominant plant, but an amazing variety of shapes and colors. All competing? Or is it all living in harmony like thousands of contented holidaymakers on a beach - without a policeman in sight.

Could it be that geneticists have become mesmerized by the raw code of the genes, just as I had once been mesmerized by grids, anodes and cathodes meaninglessly bouncing around before "luck" caused them to become fused together as functioning thermionic valves?

Perhaps it is impossible for us to truly understand the reasons for the universe's existence, for how can we expect the design itself, you and me, to recognize the designer's intent? Can a pot know why the potter formed it?

Evolution is a belief system that is still relatively undeveloped. By undeveloped I mean that in general, only the negative characteristics such as "the survival of the fittest", are highlighted in classical evolutionary theory. Yet, when I observe young animal life, such as a feeding blackbird fledgling, it flutters subserviently and humbly towards its parents – and the parents respond with gifts of food. Care, compassion and a simple form of altruism seem to me to be instinctive, built into all life. It is only when fledglings become over demanding or aggressive that they are chased away. Although some form of evolution may work without aggression, there is no way it would work without cooperation; even the simple sex act normally involves cooperation!

What then of a manifestation of the pure joy of an interacting commonality, an interdependence, a familiar comfort, a comradeship, a companionable existence with others, giving sheer pleasure,

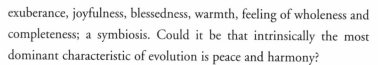

exuberance, joyfulness, blessedness, warmth, feeling of wholeness and completeness; a symbiosis. Could it be that intrinsically the most dominant characteristic of evolution is peace and harmony?

Scientists are motivated and excited by the joy of discovery, and artists are driven by an internal fire to express themselves.

A child crawls as an urge to reach an object; at first it does not consciously know why the waving of its arms and legs are able to move its whole body forward. Initially it is not aware of any of its actions, only the inner, burning drive to reach its destination. But built in is a mechanism which learns the movement and makes it deliberate; to conform to the will of the child. The child's motivation and determination overcomes the inertia of the body, which appears to only want to eat, sleep and defecate. The child's will forces the body to move in a coordinated way. It is the "self" of the child that takes over many of the body's movements, from crawling to speech, and it is the "self" that interacts with human consciousness and can change to become a greater Self, as we will see later.

A mountaineer may follow a false trail, but still be motivated to keep trying to reach the objective. Even if the final destination is shrouded in a blanketing mist, climbers who believe in mountain peaks will keep trying to scale the heights. And if many try, a series of synchronistic events could occur ensuring that one ultimately succeeds. So it could be with evolutionary processes, which are the result of synchronistic synergies that change one level of complexity, through harmony and cooperation, to a new and more advanced form of complexity. Cells do not need to know where they are going, only that they want to experience more. Chance, and aggression, could well decree which particular cell evolves. But the parallel, inner cooperative characteristic of evolution decrees that one definitely will.

There is an inbuilt adaptability waiting to burst into life, as the spring blossoms with the warming sun.

At all stages the universe generates excess for the next level of its development: like a great ship of war, bristling with many types of armament ready for action; like a tiger pacing back and forth behind the bars of his cage in the middle of London's Regents Park, longing for more, we, like the tiger, often feel the urge to escape, to move on, even if we do not understand just where the move may take us.

Each level of complexity has built in redundancy, primed ready for the next possible external triggering event. There are many types of atoms with countless possible combinations. We are aware of hundreds of thousand of types of proteins. There are whole hosts of unicellular life and a myriad of multi-cellular life forms. The Welsh countryside teems with plant variety, as do the great plains of Africa with its fabulous animal life. There is even excess capacity built in to our brains, with an over abundance of neurons.

Where does this drive to have built in superfluity, redundancy and motivation come from? Why does it all happen? Why isn't a simple level of evolution enough?

It is beginning to appear more logical that intelligence is, after all, built into the whole process of evolution!

Could it be that the ancient seers and prophets already knew about what we call the Big Bang and evolution, and recorded these things in their scriptures, perhaps in the form of analogies? One such record is in the book of Genesis where it is recorded that creation was completed in six days, "By the seventh day God had finished the work he had been doing ... " By suggesting that a few billion earth-years is but a day in the life of God, the creation, and the whole of evolution could deem to have happened in, "Six God days".

We cannot be dominated by our emotions and preconceived ideas and eliminate intelligence and God from the story of evolution if we are seeking nothing but the truth.

Could it be that the barrier that prevents a deeper understanding of our human condition stems from within our own fears? Are scientists afraid of agreeing that intelligence is part of evolution; might egos be dented by appearing to agree with some of the ideas to be found within religion? Are religious groups afraid that if they admit to the truths uncovered by science they will deny God? Many of us, it seems, set up simple arguments for marginal aspects of other people's beliefs, and then, with great gusto, refute them. In order to move on it would be good if we agree that there is integrity to be found in many discoveries, theories and beliefs which may not be our own.

It is perfectly rational to believe in God, and in the concept of evolution. Logical thought and emotional enthusiasm aren't necessarily at odds. What could be more awesome than Crick and Watson discovering the double helix of the life, or a mathematician deriving a formula to explain the origin of the universe, or a scientist finding life on Mars? Hearts will pound; pulses will race. It has even been know for sober philosophers to dance in naked abandonment down a public street shouting *eureka*. So why are so many scientists and others skeptical of a group of "happy clappy" Christian believers, or of the exuberant expression of the Hindu, or the abandoned dancing of the Dervishes. They, too, may have been led to discover a great truth.

Within the lives of animals and ourselves there is the pleasure of fresh food, the joy of sex, the mothering love that protects and nourishes the next generation. Is this then the purpose of life, to find temporary pleasure and enjoyment and then, like a spring flower, wither and die? All these goals and possessions are transient; all will fade with the passing of time; all will become as nothing. Even if we consider ourselves as procreating animals making the world ecologically sound for future generations, there is no permanent meaning for life, for even *these* things, noble as they are, will in time fade and disappear.

In wandering a little way down this scientific Garden of Eden, I hope that you agree with me that evolution is an excellent theory, focusing our minds on many intriguing possibilities. However, these ideas, theories and hypotheses leave us with overwhelming gaps, and demand that we have unbelievable leaps of faith, if we are to agree with many of their underlying assumptions.

I believe that if we wish to know our destiny we will always have to keep open minds and move away from the comfort zone of simply accumulating wealth, ideas and philosophies; otherwise we could be in danger of losing our only chance to influence our ultimate destiny, for it could turn out that this existence is the only opportunity, the only gift, of life that we ever have.

We will now slip a little further into the world of science; a science of interaction, oneness and connectiveness. As we do so we will have to proceed with care for, as our island of knowledge grows bigger, I expect that the shoreline of spectacular, hypnotic and self-satisfying wonder will increase, making it difficult to maintain a focus on our ultimate destiny.

CHAPTER 2

THE LAND OF SCIENCE

PATTERNS AND PREDICTIONS IN SCIENCE

LIFE IS NOT bound by the limitations of evolutionary theory. There is more to life than science alone can unveil, especially concerning the purpose of our lives. But, can some of our modern scientific discoveries and ideas point out to us which way we should travel to reach our destiny?

Science is certainly helping us to uncover a complex universe filled with a kaleidoscope of wonders.

In the early years of my engineering career the awesome possibilities of science began to blossom for me, especially when I was first confronted with rooms filled with gleaming metal levers, rotating discs and giant stainless steel ball bearings; all moving with synchronized precision. Those fascinating rooms were actually filled with Second World War "predictors", unsurpassed at the time for their ability to calculate the optimum trajectory for anti-aircraft shells. Science today has moved a long way from those early aids to war. One day we may even witness a smart missile homing in on a selected individual by locking onto his or her unique DNA signature. Will such things help us to survive, or will they spell disaster for the whole of our human race? How can we know?

Over the last few hundred years the successful application of modern science has brought comfort and pleasure to many. In

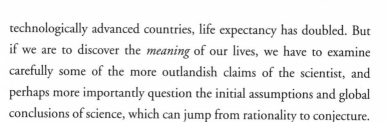

technologically advanced countries, life expectancy has doubled. But if we are to discover the *meaning* of our lives, we have to examine carefully some of the more outlandish claims of the scientist, and perhaps more importantly question the initial assumptions and global conclusions of science, which can jump from rationality to conjecture. Are the most established theories *nothing but the truth?*

In the first chapter, we came across many concepts that at first sight seemed to be scientifically sound. Yet often these theories were not backed up with direct experimental proof, but rather by calculations, observations and experiments that *implied* the desired theory had been verified. They were, in fact, only an accumulation of information more properly called secondary proof. In practice, observing such things as 'sticky red stuff' heralds a plethora of possibilities from which it is possible for us to conjecture what it actually is - blood if it's in a horror movie, jam if it's on toast! It is human logic, enthusiasm and assumption that is used to interpret what observed results signify. Regrettably, some scientists, and even more so the media, all too quickly impose their own preferred solution. They may be on the right track, but too often they are making assumptions based upon their predisposed beliefs, or a yearning to make an impact.

What then, does it take for a scientific theory to become accepted as a proven fact? Well, it turns out that there are only two paradigms to consider when it comes to proof. Both have a spectrum of possibilities; both can be defined by their extremities.

The first paradigm concerns just how directly the experiment reproduces the real world, i.e. that which actually occurs. The two extremes of this paradigm are defined by asking if the experiment can be considered as a primary proof (i.e. is it a direct, reproducible correlation of the real world?), or a secondary proof (is it a proof which only indirectly implies the real world?).

Direct reproducible proofs, primary proofs, demonstrate the

actual theory being proposed. They are not proofs from which we have to make inferences. Letting go of an apple always results in it falling towards the centre of the earth, which proves that there is an attraction between an apple and Earth. It will happen time after time after time, it can, at any time, be shown to be universally true by directly demonstrating the phenomena. This Apple-Earth experiment constitutes a direct proof.

By further experiments just above the Earth's surface we may well directly verify the force of gravity and derive equations to tell us the speed and acceleration that the apple would undergo when we released it at some future time. But no matter how sophisticated our measurements, we would never *know with absolute certainty* what would be the fate of an apple released near the Moon's surface unless we actually tried it. Without actually going to the Moon and dropping the apple it would always remain a theory. It was not until 1969 when Neil Armstrong took that giant step for mankind onto the Moon's surface that the theory of gravity on the moon was truly vindicated.

How different this all is to the theories concerning the origin of the universe and life. In this context only secondary measurements are possible, giving us only very remote and indirect proof. For unlike our Apple-Moon experiment, the origin of the universe can never be demonstrated for the simple reason that we will never be able to start with nothing and take fifteen billion years over an experiment. We cannot directly demonstrate evolution from atoms and molecules to amoebae and Homo sapiens. Theories such as the Big Bang and evolution are a great help for scientists, engineers, mathematicians and technologists when they explore our universe. They are used to design experiments that evaluate more and more of the awesome jigsaw of our physical universe. Although these theories never seem to tell us anything meaningful about our purpose or our place in that awesomeness, they are exciting, and often result in many beneficial discoveries.

There is today an over abundance of scientific assumptions,

indirect second order proofs which are often confused with the rigors of direct scientifically demonstrable proof. This indirect proof, by its very nature, cannot unequivocally verify any theory. It is a once removed proof. It is like seeing ripples on a dark, still pond, then ignoring all possibilities for the ripples other than a cherished theory or belief. We become like fishermen who are convinced that all ripples are caused by great fish, lurking just below the surface. Darwin's *natural selection* evolutionary theory relies on indirect proof. A proof that advocates the rationale of evolution and change, but in no way eliminates the possibility of an underlying intelligence, an overriding purpose or the possibility of a more profound reason for the evolution of complexity.

Evolution is a superb working hypothesis, even if an intelligent source, preordained evolution by ensuring that the underlying characteristics of matter, time and space, *automatically* allowed for the emergence of life. It is an excellent vehicle for the present, but it would be well to remember that it could turn out to be another flat earth theory, or like the belief that the heavens revolved around our planet, Earth. Even so, flat earth theories helped early mariners to navigate coastal waters and to begin exploring sea travel!

It is easy to become hypnotized by numerous charismatic scientists who tell us that secondary, indirect evidence constitutes absolute proof! Much, if not all, of our understanding of astronomy, cosmology, evolution and recorded human history is based on indirect, secondary evidence. This means that we should not take our records as being factual, but rather as well founded suggestions and working hypotheses that help us to uncover nature's secrets.

As well as direct and indirect proof there is the second paradigm of proof to explore. Simply stated it is the fact that all proof is through the experience of either ourselves personally (first-person experience) or by someone else (third-person experience). Like being told that from the hotel to the beach is a five-minute walk, but when you actually walk it yourself it takes a minimum of fifteen minutes. The five minutes is the third-person "proof", the fifteen is for you a first- person "proof". And in general, our own experience is to be preferred as a true reflection of the real world. However, a third-person experience is usually accepted as being true when many people independently carry out procedures that support a particular theory. To increase our belief in the truth of any seemingly factual encounter independence of the source is essential. It is this independence that must be examined with care.

In the world of science sometimes, due to poorly controlled experiment or incorrect interpretation of results, scientific "facts" are in time shown to be incorrect and have to be modified. But, always we find that the most powerful proof (although not the most persuasive for others) is not third party but first-party proof. To see the birth of a chick and wait for its bedraggled body to become beautiful is a vastly superior proof than any number of people telling you that eggs contain bright fluffy life forms. The best proof is always in experiencing phenomena for ourselves. Of course we must beware of such things as magicians mirrors, lights, non-visual black threads, hidden microphones and so on. Tricks or poor science will not do!

To sum up then, a vast amount of literature has been produced about proof and truth; even so, it all boils down to just two fundamental paradigms. The first asks the question, "Is it a direct, primary, or an indirect, secondary, proof that we are talking of?" The second paradigm concerns us personally, "Did we directly experience the phenomena for ourselves, or has it been reported to us by others?"

These are the universals of all proof.

They mean that we can only increase our own belief in two ways. Firstly by having the experience ourselves (moving the proof from a third person to a first-person experience). Secondly by replacing indirect proof by direct proof. In practice, however, moving to a first-person experience and/or a direct experimental proof may prove to be difficult or even impossible, such as "proving" evolution is an undisputed fact.

It should come as no surprise to us that both the scientist and the religiously inclined frequently tell us that their theories are based upon direct, first-person proof, when in practice, they are all too often based upon theories, revered writings, visions, innovations, hunches and ideas and many other secondary proofs.

Is it then possible for any form of science to help us in the search for our destiny? Well yes, I believe that it does offer us some very important clues. This can be seen quite clearly when we consider first-order proof, illustrating the importance of truth, for false claims concerning demonstrable proof are inevitably superseded. To find our destiny we must be willing to sacrifice many cherished ideas and beliefs and seek only truth.

Bearing this in mind, how far then can we apply scientific method and logic to evaluate such complex subjects as connectiveness, individuality and freedom?

INTERCONNECTEDNESS

I FIND IT hard to believe that it is well over forty years since Dicky Stephens, Clive Rees and myself set out to find the mystical, ruff-collared bird that we had heard existed somewhere in Wales. We cycled off on our uncharted journey with little knowledge of where to go; we possessed nothing remotely as sophisticated as a map. We had very little money, no food, nothing to drink, not even any waterproof clothing let alone a tent, yet we fully expected to be successful.

For a large part of a sun-dappled day we glided through the silver-tinted Usk valley protected by familiar woodlands and comforting hills. We happened on a warm barn filled with welcoming bright yellow straw. The following morning with straw needles still embedded in our clothes we stood, many miles from home, at the waters edge of Langorse lake in rapt awe, speechlessly staring at the bobbing, diving, magical color and form of a fully ruffed Great Crested Grebe.

Was finding the barn, the lake and the Grebe pure luck, or were we part of something greater? Had a form of simple spiritual tuning of our minds occurred? Had we invoked instinctive knowledge that we all, at times, feel we possess as we journey through life? Could we all, in some way, be interconnected with each other and to the universe, as quantum mechanics predicts, by "entanglement"? Many religious movements, alternative and complementary medical

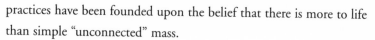

practices have been founded upon the belief that there is more to life than simple "unconnected" mass.

Science tells us of matter "popping in and out of space" and an existence which is within a continuum, and we are part of this continuum. If this is true, then we exist as part of a congealed reality that only lasts for a few moments of cosmological time.

Einstein clearly showed a universal interconnectedness between entities such as electrons. If electrons that had been previously combined in the same molecule were separated, they showed a mysterious, non-causal connection. In other words, associated particles that are later moved any distance apart, are linked in such a way that if you change the spin of one of these particles, the other particle will simultaneously change its own spin. Einstein's work tells us that particles are, in fact, not particles but intense fields that move through space as a whole. Such distributed pulses do not end abruptly, but spread out to large distances with decreasing intensity, implying that the entire universe has to be understood as a single undivided whole.

This amazing discovery of Einstein's is being enhanced and verified by today's science. What is even more amazing is that this concept is implied in the ancient writings of the Hindu Vedantic scriptures.

The seers who produced these early Hindu scriptures believed that God created the universe out of himself. They believed that God is all pervasive, everywhere. Like the finest of fine particles, God's resonance gave rarefactions and concentrations, becoming focused so that great vortexes and galaxies were impressed upon the void. The concentration increased and burning masses were produced with whirling planets. The focusing intensified and life erupted. Then, as the focusing, whirling, "fading and establishing" became more and more concentrated, individual consciousness was born.

To state the same concept in more Western terms, the

universe may be considered as patterns originating in the mind of God. This was succinctly recorded over one thousand nine hundred years ago in Paul's letter to the Colossians, "In him everything in heaven and on earth was created, not only things visible but also the invisible orders of thrones, sovereignties, authorities, and powers: the whole universe has been created through him". Some go as far as suggesting that the universe was not simply conceived by God but is the actual mind of God.

You may take a more scientific view of quantum "entanglement", such as the one reported in the *New Scientist* on the 29th September 2001, "Clouds of trillions of atoms have for the first time been linked by quantum 'entanglement' – that spooky, almost telepathic link between distant particles. The feat opens new possibilities for quantum communication systems and sci-fi style teleporting of objects from one place to another."

David Bohm has taken Einstein's experiments further by developing some excellent illustrations for what he called "enfoldment". Some of his best are the "holographic plate" and the "ink spot". The latter uses a transparent cylinder full of a viscous fluid, such as clear, thick oil, into which a drop of ink is introduced. The ink is put into the fluid while it is carefully stirred in one direction. The ink drop gradually transforms into a thread that extends around the whole cylinder, a shade of grey. If the fluid is later carefully stirred in the opposite direction, the transformation is reversed, and the droplet of ink reappears, reconstituted. The fact that the ink spot is always present points to a reality that could be like lumps emerging from a multi-dimensional soup; a reality more the result of a constant, interconnected movement than numerous static unconnected "blobs". This, in turn, implies that everything is in some way connected to everything else.

This very exciting model of the universe is open, dynamic, interconnected and full of living qualities. Matter is seen as sometimes particles, sometimes waves, sometimes mass, sometimes energy; all interconnected and constantly in motion. Interconnectedness could well be the common principle underlying homeopathy, telepathy, clairvoyance, precognition, prophesy and such things as a feeling of *déjà vu,* or of being in the right place at the right time, along with other "spiritual states" that we will be meeting later. Perhaps you have on times, even been accosted by that strange phenomenon of being aware of future events, often seemingly trivial and yet not easily explained by science.

Enfoldment and interconnectedness give support to the concept of synchronicity, where positive events occur in our lives and click into place, giving us a feeling of general well-being.

Even everyday things can seem, at first, to be extraordinary. For example, the social psychologist Stanley Milgram performed an experiment in 1967 that showed that everyone in the world knows everyone else through just a few intermediaries. An effect termed, "The six degrees of separation". In other words I could talk to someone I meet, and that conversation could be relayed to the president of the USA on one hand or an African Bushman on the other, with only four intermediaries between me and either of them! At first this sounds incredible, until we recollect the amount of intercontinental travel and communication that takes place today.

I find that some days I am filled with energetic enthusiasm and throughout the day things seemed to drop into place with little or no effort; days of truly positive synchronistic encounters; days that my wife, Jeanette, calls "Indian Days", after our travels in India in 1988. At other times the opposite is true and I would have achieved far more by staying in bed all day!

One such example of synchronicity occurred when I revisited the Isle of Man after a fifty-year absence. While there I decided that, this time, I would see for myself the famous native tailless, Manx cat. Jeanette and I searched in vain for the elusive feline. And then unexpectedly it came into my mind that I had to go to a church. Off we drove for several miles to the nearest church and went through the churchyard with a fine toothcomb. No cat anywhere. Disappointed I was about to leave when I saw a lady coming towards us with a bunch of keys. We explained our quest and she said the organist who was practicing in the church at that moment had a Manx cat! In no time we were enjoying a cup of tea and biscuits in this kind lady's home, while stroking a genuine, born-tailless Manx cat!

An even more puzzling event occurred, many years ago. Jeanette and I were having a weekend break in a small village in mid-Wales. The only evening entertainment, other than the usual pub was a cup of tea and a Christmas mince pie organized by the local church in aid of charity. The highlight of the evening was to be a "grand draw". Everyone had purchased raffle tickets as a contribution to the charity, and now the winning numbers were about to be pulled out from the proverbial hat. We were at a table with half a dozen other middle class, respectable ladies, when I had an uncontrollable urge to tell "Jane", as I will call her, that she would win the "botanical garden", enclosed in a large two-foot diameter spherical jar. She smiled and said politely that there would be no room on her little cottage window for such a large display. Ticket numbers were called out until there was only one prize left – the botanical garden. The last number was drawn from the hat and a gentleman from a remote part of the room walked over to collect his prize. So my overwhelming feeling had been wrong! Then to my surprise the man stopped in mid stride, smiled, waved his hand disconcertingly and with an air of great sacrifice said, "Take another ticket from the hat", and still smiling he returned to his seat. And so the grand finale was re-run. This time, just before the winning number was announced, I saw one of Jane's tickets visibly glow and mechanically I called out the number just before the final call. There was laughter on our table at the coincidence of my predictions, but then unlike me, they had not seen that ticket glow!

If anyone else had explained the events above to me, I may well have replied that their memory must have been playing tricks with them. But this is not an answer that I can give to myself. I *know* that I had been given some unexplainable forewarning of that evening's events.

The seemingly meaningful coincidence of two or more events has always been part of humanity's ancient beliefs. Beliefs, which invoke the holistic, synchronistic, interconnected universe by performing a sacred dance, a religious sacrifice, prophesying, healing or intercessionary prayers.

What a strange notion synchronicity and enfoldment is for a person like me who believes in my individuality. Yet I have experienced "oneness" many times. I have been not just an observer, but part of the sheer magical beauty of natural settings – from razor-sharp mountain peaks cutting into rose-filled evening skies, to the soft, green bosom of fertile valleys nourishing their teeming life. I have been conscious of my mind free-falling through the enchantment of great music. Yes, I have been blessed many times, drifting like a cloud of pure universal love within what I can only call "pre-existing interconnected cosmic joy".

It is during moments such as these that it is possible to feel, to be part of the All, that Oneness which is all creation, and to glimpse truths that are to be found in simple words such as the Chinese saying, "If you cut a blade of grass, you shake the universe".

Could interconnected synchronicity be our complete destiny, with nothing of our individuality having lasting value? Or could it be that the thick syrup of universal oneness still allows us to be free-thinking individuals, with a purpose which can be achieved, at least in part, by our own efforts?

INDIVIDUALITY

DO WE EVER make a choice, or are the laws of cause and effect governing all our actions? Are all our thoughts and actions simply predetermined responses to the demands of our surroundings, our built in personalities and our previous experiences?

If the stars, our genes, our social environment, our karma, God, or even the devil predetermine our lives, then we are simply reacting automatically like amoebae moving from acid water into neutrality. If this were the case, we would be agreeing with Benedictus de Spinoza (1632-77), Gottfried Wilhelm Leibniz (1646-1716) and that great mathematical astronomer Pierre Simon de Laplace (1740-1827), who reasoned that if they knew the present state of the world, they could predict the future in its entirety. This theory results in an interpretation of life as nothing more than a series of prearranged events.

If their logic is correct then we have absolutely no freedom of choice. We are simply on a meaningless conveyor belt that transports us from birth to death.

However, it seems to me much more likely that we do, at least in part, have some degree of choice, not only because of my own sense of individuality, but also because I have observed for myself that even simple life forms appear to exhibit a degree of freedom of choice.

Take as an example a typical settled colony of one of the

8,000 species of ants. At first sight a regimented column of ants appears to leave absolutely no freedom for the individual to choose its destiny. But, closer inspection indicates that an ant can, at times, decide for itself what to do next. For example, if a worker ant is out foraging for food and comes across signs implying that there are sufficient ants around for the job in hand it will, of its own inclination, go and look for a different job. The total pheromone trails left by other ants, that our dedicated little worker encounters, encourages it to move on. And it is this triggered choice of professions by individual ants that brings about the creation of Ant City. This is not what I expected at all. I had envisaged a form of top-down management structure along the lines of one of our global multinationals. Ant City however, hums with smooth efficiency in its highly organized routine, without an overseer in sight! Surely each ant has a form of individuality, a freedom of choice?

Ant cooperation illustrates the relatively new science of "emergence", where hierarchies and complexity develop from simplicity. "Simple" ants create a city with food stores, incubation rooms, gardens, burial grounds and rubbish tips. But in no way am I, or modern science, the first to observe the individuality of the ant and its limited, but nevertheless freedom of choice, for it is over two and a half thousand years since Biblical writers recorded, "Go to the ant, … observe her ways and gain wisdom. She has no prince, no governor, or ruler." (*Proverbs* 5:6,7 REB).

Today many scientists and technologists use a set of simple choices within independent parts of a software program to create complex results. That is, they use the principles of emergence to design lucrative, interactive, self-learning computer games, and for simulating social behavior to evaluate such things as the effect of town planning on urban environments. Super computer programs based upon our understanding of ant colonies have been used for films such as *The Matrix* and *Lord of the Rings,* especially the latter's Middle

Earth battles. Here fifty thousand soldiers are not actors or puppets but eighty types of software extras each type with several fixed characteristics. Using techniques such as "fuzzy logic", each individual appears to have its own brain as it responds to external stimuli.. Soldiers in the centre of an attack act differently to those on the outside, all very reminiscent of real warfare.

The emergence of complexity from simplicity exists everywhere there is a life form, from the simplest, seemingly mindless, gathering together of garden slime moulds to the most complex and advanced human groups such as the Greenham Common protester in England, against the use of nuclear weapons in the 1980s. By their selfless sincerity those Greenham Common women influenced events that eventually lead to the historic dismantling of the Berlin Wall in Germany.

Over the years I have been part of many different forms of human activities and joined many different groups and other societies. But, the question remains, "Is it really *me* making the choices?" Do *I* have sufficient free choice to influence and change my destiny? Although I cannot always avoid pain, can I avoid the mental anguish of suffering? Is it inevitable for me to exhibit a measure of selfishness and guilt when I enjoy food, sex or simply lying in the sun?

I am the same *me* now as I was in my schoolboy photo. I am the spark which in essence is unchanging yet is dynamic, moving, growing, learning, experiencing and becoming that which represents the permanent in myself. It is this *me* that needs to have freedom to experience, to develop and to learn to live through both the pleasures and the pains of life. Comprehending *being* is the basis of many belief systems. The ancient Hindu scripture, the Mundaka Upanishad records a relationship between *being* and Self, "The Self is not to be known through study of the scriptures, nor through subtlety of the intellect, nor though much learning. But by him who longs for him is he known. Verily unto him does the Self reveal his true being... The

Self is not to be known by the weak, nor by the thoughtless nor by those who do not rightly meditate. But by the rightly meditative, the thoughtful, and the strong, he is fully known." I would add that, it is not to be known by a third party even if he or she used the most sophisticated brain scan on a person who claimed to be experiencing *being* or Self. These things are only known by direct personal experience.

It is this uniqueness, which is *me*, that is surrounded by, and reacts with, a very physical world. My life is part of the rhythm, the hum, the silent pulse of the universe in which I exist. Wordsworth was expressing the essence of *being* when he wrote in *I wondered lonely as a cloud* "They flash upon that inward eye which is the bliss of solitude".

It is the inward eye that develops when we contemplate the images of the world in which we find ourselves. And this is why, in so many world scriptures, we are encouraged to find a quiet place, to be alone. The Gospel of Saint Matthew (6:6) says, "But when you pray go into a room by yourself, shut the door, and pray to your Father in secret". In practice I had to either rise before the start of the clamor of a working day or turn off the whole paraphernalia of electrical gadgets, including doorbells, telephones, TV, computers and microwave cookers before true meditative prayer came to me – but more of this later.

I find it childishly exciting to think, that not only are we separate and independent individuals, who together can produce great complexity, but that we are also part of that awesome wholeness which is the holistic, ever-changing universe itself.

FREE TO CHOOSE

LOOKING DEEPER INTO predestination and freewill it is apparent that while political and social freedoms are very important indeed, personal freedom is paramount. It is what goes on inside our mind that is the true measure of our freedom.

The human brain is a form of machine that has amazing and unsurpassed complexity. It can generate outcomes that cannot be known by simply measuring the data going in. The outcome is not always predictable, implying that original ideas can be generated in the brain itself. If we can generate our own ideas, then it could well be possible to influence our future, and possible to change our outlook on life. This simple logic indicates the possibility of freedom of thought.

Our freedom is subjected to many limitations. Paul grappled with this when he wrote his letter to the Romans (7:19-20) nearly two-thousand years ago, "The good which I want to do, I fail to do; but what I do is the wrong which is against my will, clearly it is no longer I who am the agent, but sin that has its dwelling in me." I'm not sure just how far we can blame a separate entity "sin" for our actions, but there is little doubt that we all experience inner conflicts and limitations when making decisions.

I vividly remember a simple, yet for me at the time a dramatic, incident that occurred early one summer morning in 1970. I was just one, in an army of thousands, six abreast, walking briskly over London Bridge into the sleepy City of London. Just another insignificant, dark suited figure. But, that day I was filled with the exhilarating glow of youthful success. *Reuters News* had recently agreed a lucrative consultancy contract with my company, and I was out to make a killing. Then, quite abruptly, from deep within my mind's eye there flashed before me a scene invoking true exhilaration. It was of the open, sun–splashed, golden hillsides of my youth in my homeland of Wales. Tumbling doubts of meaninglessness flooded into my thoughts. Dazed, I froze and stood still. Then slowly I became aware of droplets of humanity obligingly parting and reforming around my motionless figure. I felt as if I had become a rock parting the murmuring waters of a mountain stream.

I had suddenly found it difficult, even painful, to conform and simply be one of the "lemmings" marching into the financial hub of the great slumbering City. Did I stop walking of my own free choice, or was I simply responding to genetically induced patterns in my mind, some inevitable pre-destined program?

There are numerous events in our lives that point to our lack of freedom of action. For example, many years ago, overnight, I became completely deaf in one ear, lost all sense of balance, and had what seemed to be a mammoth lorry continually revving up its engine in my head. I certainly didn't choose that experience! As my suffering gradually reduced I became more aware of the suffering and degradation of countless millions throughout the world, their different levels of joys and sorrows reflecting many preordained levels of freedom. So much outside their sphere of influence - I would not expect anyone to choose to be born blind or deaf or crippled.

Reflecting on my experiences I find that freedom is beginning to appear more like a spectrum of possibilities. At one end of the spectrum all is deterministic, we have no choice, while at the other end we seem to enter into the realm of a limited freedom of thought and action.

One of the more enlightened concepts, concerning predestation and freewill, was told to me by Swami Dayatmananda. I had first met Swami Dayatmananda when he had arrived in Britain from India in the early 1990s. At the time he looked very small and cold. By 1996 he was in charge of the Vedanta Centre at Bourne End exuding confidence, mild countenance and quiet wisdom. He listened to my thoughts on freewill before nudging me towards a way forward beyond the dichotomy that I saw between the absolute knowledge of an omniscient God, and a concept of human freewill. He simply said, "For God all things have already been played out and thus in that way it is predestination. For us, we do not know, therefore we have choice and we are free to choose".

By putting God on a different plain and suggesting a logic of predestination from the point of view of God, and freewill from the point of view of mankind, he was giving my mind a glimmer of understanding. The Swami was implying that because the human mind could not encompass the mind of God, freewill and predestination should only be considered as a peripheral debate.

At least we appear to be able to choose to believe that we have free choice rather than choose to believe that we have none. For me to assume that all is pre-destined is a fatalistic view of the world, which is completely unverifiable and adds nothing to life's adventure. Surely it is better to assume that we have freewill and to go on to consider the possibility of changing some of our thoughts and actions that could ultimately affect our destiny. Can we alter the way in which we perceive our lives, by the development and refinement of our own minds? And in so doing find clues as to why we are here. This approach was certainly taught by the Buddha some two and a half thousand years ago, when he opposed some of his own philosophy of simple deterministic cause and effect by saying, "Wisdom can be cultivated. It comes into being through a set of conditions, conditions that we have the power to develop. These conditions are actually

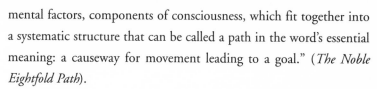

mental factors, components of consciousness, which fit together into a systematic structure that can be called a path in the word's essential meaning: a causeway for movement leading to a goal." (*The Noble Eightfold Path*).

Could it be that all things that seem to be predetermined, that are unalterable and subject to blind chance, are only the surface, superficial things of life and that they have no deep meaning in the search for our destiny?

I believe that we are not only conditioned by the workings of our minds, our social grouping and our interaction with the world, we are also able to influence our destiny. Whether we choose to go "left" or "right" can make a profound difference to the rest of our lives.

It seems to me that it is through free choice that my inner self is being changed. I will always have to be on my guard, for any change in my character could become permanent; one choice laying the foundation for the next choice, and so on. This implies that the childish, exploratory, acts of killing insects or stealing apples might lead to a life of violence and crime, but fortunately it is far more likely that these simple choices cause us to reflect, and lead us to more worthwhile pastimes. Much depends on the response of the society in which we live.

No matter how significant, or insignificant our choice, it is through freedom to choose that our consciousness begins to develop.

Every time we enact our thoughts, our memories are altered and with them our developing consciousness. The more we practice deceit the more difficult it becomes to live an open life. The more we seek to face the world with altruistic love, the more loving a person we become. The choices we make today will affect the choices we make tomorrow.

In the space afforded to each of us by the advance of science and the effective use of the world's energy, a sobering thought that may help us to concentrate our minds is that, sooner or later, we will leave life's maze and pass through the door of death. Even our best friends and relatives will only be able to stand by and watch, as we, completely and utterly alone, go through that final door.

There are many ideas concerning what happens the other side of the door of death. Many scientists, along with humanists and other groups, believe that birth and death are, in effect like two huge, impenetrable steel doors. Could some people have superb logic and intelligence yet never experience, or cannot remember, a special moment, transcendental moment, when the doors of life momentarily open? For them a deeper sense of *being* does not appear to exist, and many only encounter experiences that reflect back to them the majesty of their own minds.

I doubt if many people who are born blind, who may well have had profound transcendental experiences, would attempt to evaluate great paintings, for they would be aware of their inability in that particular field of human knowledge. Yet, many with no experience of the transcendental, the gift of the grace of God, or any from of spiritual awareness still insist they know it all, and often with great flamboyance and linguistic ability, confidently give bland, uninformed answers about the meaning of life and human destiny.

It appears that science can only offer us intelligent guesses, based upon the physical world of atoms, genes, change and decay. Guesses that may always be ignorant of the transcendental part of our human condition. However, religions give us other explanations; some inform us that we will have many lives and our goal is the perfect peace of Nirvana. Others tell us that we are destined for a heaven or damned to exist in the torment and pain of hell. While still others suggest that we will be reunited with our ancestors. There are many concepts and combinations, but whatever the truth turns out to be, there is little doubt that understanding the spiritual, the transcendental, dimension of our human condition will be our only companion as we enter our own personal door of death ... in which case we would be foolish if we did not fully explore any possible transcendental reality, for such knowledge may well be the golden key that opens to us an understanding of our ultimate destiny.

What then are the overall messages that we can take from the world of science and technology? They have certainly allowed us to achieve astonishing things: create complex worldwide communication networks, burst out beyond our atmosphere to explore new worlds, look into the awesome majesty of distant galaxies so that we may now have witnessed the beginning of time. We have even entered the strange world of subatomic particles, and begun the long journey of unraveling the magnificent complexity of the living cell. So many new inroads which, with wisdom and patience, may eventually benefit the whole bio-system of our earthly home and bring joy to future generations.

But science and technology seems to have little to say about the reality of God. It seems as if the universe have presented humanity with huge amounts of data to unravel, which has distracted scientists from their place within it. In general they have become too busy measuring the material world to be aware of the spirit within the cloth, and even if the spirit were measured, many scientists would consider it as part of the material and fail to recognize its true significance.

The detailed discoveries of science, like all worldly trappings, will not form part of our *ultimate* destiny. However, science clearly teaches us that it is only by seeking truth, not lies and deceit, that we will eventually uncover the facts about our physical world. This yearning for truth is surely the most important message for us to take from the land of science.

As well as illustrating the importance of truth, the other great gift of science has been to give many more of us a surplus of time, beyond our daily struggle to survive, and for many, scientific achievements have increased life expectancy. With a surplus of time we can increase our worldly goals; own a bigger car, live in a grander house, be part of a larger social circle, sit for yet another hour watching TV, or we can use it for more ethical and transcendental goals.

So, the question is, "Do we agree with the Buddha when he advocates improving our own wisdom through cultivating a deeper understanding of our self and our world?" It seems to me that we can, and moreover, we should be able to utilize the importance of truth, and the free time that science and technology have given us to continue our journey. First then, we will venture into the world of the conscious mind with the aim of uncovering possible evidence that we can later apply to our daily lives.

PART II

EXPERIENCE

CHAPTER 3

THE LAND OF CONSCIOUSNESS

JUST A THOUGHT

WHAT IS *ME*? Who am I? How do I know *me*? At first these questions seem childishly simple, yet when we attempt to answer such questions we seem to descend into a fog and then it becomes all too easy to return to the mesmerizing world of things, events and human emotional interaction. Saint Augustine of Hippo succinctly describes the problem:

> "People travel to wonder at the heights of the
> mountains,
> at the huge waves of the sea,
> at the long courses of rivers,
> at the vast compass of the ocean.
> At the circular motion of the stars
> yet they pass themselves by without wondering."

It is through understanding ourselves that we are better able to know the world, and in turn this understanding depends upon our brains, minds and consciousness.

Science is making many inroads into understanding the electro-magnetic-chemical activities of the brain, and is beginning to link these essentially physical activities, to logic, memory, emotion, empathy, insight, visions, mass hysteria, dreams, prophesy and so on.

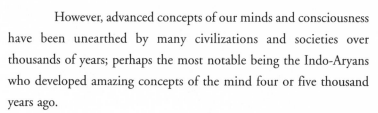

However, advanced concepts of our minds and consciousness have been unearthed by many civilizations and societies over thousands of years; perhaps the most notable being the Indo-Aryans who developed amazing concepts of the mind four or five thousand years ago.

Arguably it was the Indo-Aryans who built up the earliest great civilizations, producing the first mathematicians, the first astronomers, the first doctors and the first engineers. However, they took less interest in such things once they began to investigate the powers of the mind, consciousness and the transcendental, the latter, which they considered a *timeless* feature of existence and yet a reality with which humanity could communicate.

In other words many great civilizations before us have recognized a more permanent spirit in mankind - a dimension beyond the physical world.

As true science does not exclude the possibility of psychic or transcendental phenomena, we are then, at liberty to ask if our conscious minds, even without any signals from any of our five senses (taste, smell, touch, hearing or sight), are able to detect something which could have originated from other life forms, the cosmos, or perhaps more importantly the creative power, God.

In our search it will be good to bear in mind that there has never been any known system that can create itself without the use of an intelligence of at least one order of sophistication beyond the system itself. Take the computer world for example, no matter how sophisticated our computer world becomes it is good to remember that "intelligent" humanity started that particular little chain of events. Even though nothing has ever been known to produce itself without some form of intelligence, nevertheless it is believed by some that the mind has evolved without the need for any external intelligence.

A major problem could be the way in which that smart computer that sits on our shoulders limits us into thinking that it is itself "god". This was clearly spelt out for me by the late Swami Bhavyananda, a Hindu monk of the Ramakrishna Vedanta order, he said, "Yoga (study and management of the mind) is a difficult science. Physics and chemistry and other similar sciences are easy enough, as man has a relatively permanent unchanging thing to investigate, but in the science of yoga the field of study is the mind itself, which changes and moves and is very subtle. Here we have to study the mind with the mind, and the moment one begins, it slips."

Somehow then we have to bring together these two paradigms of understanding; *science* and the *evolved* wisdom of the ages. Are they in conflict? If we could scientifically measure all possible brain activity and brain communication would we fully understand consciousness? In particular would we be aware of our own personal consciousness as revealed through the prophets, seers and people of God?

Just how and where do thoughts arise? What is it that we are experiencing through our minds? Is it possible for our consciousness to transcend the mechanics of the brain and mind? What exactly is consciousness?

Hard questions indeed! I found that to get to grips with such difficult concepts I had to proceed with great care, one step at a time.

It was at this point that perhaps my journey really began. To make some inroads I initially assumed that the brain, located in the skull, contained our computer-like thinking processes - the mind, and that consciousness was related to our personal identity, ultimately known only to ourselves and our Creator.

THE BRAIN

SCIENCE IS FINDING it extremely difficult to locate the origin or the commencement of information flow in the brain. Some measurements even indicate that the brain seems to be able to start to react to a problem a fraction of a second before we are consciously aware that the problem even exists! This in spite of the fact that it has been estimated that even the simplest thought could involve tens of thousands of independent neurons firing, each receiving thousands of signals before they settle into a cohesive whole and a "thought" is born. However, we are still a long way from finding out just what the brain is up to. At this point in time science is not able to understand the mystery behind the decision mechanism that is taking place within each neuron, let alone understanding the subtlety of the complex activity that produces a thought.

Functionally, the brain consists of a biological neural network of a hundred billion neurons communicating with each other electrically and chemically. It is a network that grew its pathways in a unique fashion for each one of us, mainly in the womb and over the first few years of our lives. Once established, axons and dendrites that interface at the synaptic junctions causes neurons to fire when they receive a signal of about 40mV, (or 0.04 volts – around four hundred times smaller than the voltage of an average car battery).

The brain is the reference library for all our past experiences, emotions and memories. All our thinking, reasoning and perception, whether conscious or unconscious, is located in the brain. The emotions of love, hate, fear, jealously, anger and so on, which were once thought to be found in the rhythm of our heartbeat or even deep within our abdomen (a gut feeling), we now "know" are all located in the grey matter within our skulls.

What then is the brain, and how did it come to be?

The most plausible explanation of the origin of the brain, if we agree with the evolutionists, is that it has all happened rather slowly over hundreds of millions, or even billions, of years. It could well have started with a couple of nerve-like cells sidling up to one another and communicating by friendly impulses. Soon this jolly couple were noticed by other cells who began a clamor to join in the fun. As eons past more and more joined, the group changed so that a few rebellious cells became an elite and highly organized club, which took the form of an exclusive neuron town in the ectoplasm; a complexity of chattering, bossy, cells. This young exciting area is now more like the old, "down town" part of a great city, which started as a swelling at the top of the spinal chord, and is still the dominant part of the human central nervous system.

Strongman in his book *The Psychology of Emotion* refers to "down town" as the first level of brain function and explains that there are three levels of brain function - reptilian, old mammalian and new mammalian. Implying that as the brain evolved it took on more than just the functions of the physical body; it began to solve problems.

Today we have begun to map out locations within the brain, which are dedicated to specialized functions. Although the brain is amazingly versatile and adaptable, brain stimulation points to an undamaged human brain in its natural state being to some extent compartmentalized into functions such as language, movement, vision, hearing, humor, conscious thinking, emotion, meaning, and feelings. It even has a compartment that resonates when we feel that we are in the presence of God. This latter "God spot", as it is often called, can be caused to artificially resonate with electrical stimulus giving us the illusion of the presence of God that is indistinguishable from the 'real' thing. This, of course, is far from unique for artificial stimulation causes many brain and body functions to experience things that appear to be real. These things neither prove nor disprove the transcendental, but as the brain seems to exist as an objective design, i.e. each part developed for a reason, thus the "God spot" implies the reality of God rather than the opposite, as some would have us believe. Even more amazing is the research that shows some of the designated areas of the brain adapting to take on functions of an area of the brain that has become damaged.

Information passes to and from all our bodily senses to the brain, so that we cannot be considered as isolated bits of leg, arm, liver, mind and so on, but more an interacting, harmonious oneness.

Some say that the brain is far more complex than we need, and most people only use about one tenth of its capacity. If this is true the brain may have over evolved because the brain cells, neurons, were so keen to "get in on the action" - to be part of "brain city" - that they assembled in far greater numbers than we humans know how to use. On the other hand, as mentioned previously, redundancy always seems to be built into the design process behind evolution. There are more types of atoms than are required for carbon based life forms to evolve and there are more types of bacteria than needed to produce a living cell. Could it be that the brain is already primed for the development of a more advanced form of consciousness? I believe that this could well be so.

This under-utilization of the brain also allows for tremendous adaptability. A neurology professor at Cardiff University Teaching Hospital once told me that he had a patient who, through an accident, had lost almost ninety percent of his active brain cells and amazingly, within months, could function reasonably normally in society, although, as one might expect, he never regained much of his previous character.

Which leads us to ask whether the brain, including the way in which it adapts to change, is an unalterable pre-program of our genes, or whether we can consciously change it by the action of our minds alone. If our conscious minds can change the physical connections within the brain, could artificial stimulation by electrodes or magnets one day be used to program a child's brain - a brain that has been subjected to genetic manipulation? If such modifications become feasible then designer children could appear with a vengeance!

But we seem to be getting a bit too far ahead of ourselves. Our journey at this stage is to discover just what is possible for the natural mind and consciousness to achieve. Through our experiences can we consciously influence the functioning of our brains and perhaps develop our minds and consciousness in the same way that we are able to develop our bodies? Before coming to a conclusion a little more thought concerning one of the prime functions of the brain, the memory, is called for.

MEMORY

MEMORY IS WITHIN the brain. Memory represents a momentous stage of evolution. Whereas atoms, planets and solar systems, to name but a few, do not appear to remember anything of their past, and follow predetermined paths, memory allows us to learn. It gives us the possibility of changing our behavior. Without memory, we would have no freedom of choice, and consequently we would have no effect whatsoever on our destiny. Memory changes our perception, of what would otherwise appear to be random and chaotic, into an ordered, although often unpredictable, world of complexity. Often our minds develop a logic reducing complex events to understandable laws of nature.

Consider a typical experience that causes a memory to be formed. A stimulus arrives from one or more of the five primary senses (touch, smell, taste, sight and hearing) and causes two obvious types of reaction. The first is a fast track instinctive reaction, while the second is a slower measured reaction.

Put your hand on a very hot plate. Your fast track instinctive reaction will automatically pull your hand away. The second slower measured reaction may be to put your hand into something cool, and decide to be more careful with "plate contact" in future. The decision, to be wary of plates, may be modified over a period of time and could cause three things to occur: to take action (get someone else to feel the plates first), to communicate to the world (such as telling others of your dread of plates), or to do nothing. The latter, "do nothing", can in practice be a communication to oneself, which may have a bearing on, amongst other things, future decisions. You may even develop a phobia of plates!

As well as a mental experience arising from an external stimulus, new thoughts could arise spontaneously in the mind.

The memory process is largely automatic; it could be thought of as instinctive, animal behavior that accounts for a great deal of our own thoughts and actions. Simple memory could even be considered as a pre-destined response to the world.

Memories form, accumulate, get sorted, prioritized; most are discarded while many others fade with the passing of time. The totality of the memories in our brain, and their interaction, is the basis for the operation of the mind, the workhouse of all our thoughts.

There are many other subtle characteristics of memory such as the effect that hypnotic and dream experiences might have on our memories. We are in reality, voyagers, prone to a whole raft of external influences and uncontrollable mental sort-outs, turning a prodigious amount of information into a few memorable snippets of our life experiences. Chaotic randomness can easily tangle up the mind as our day progresses, especially if we become over-tired or intoxicated. Sleep seems to be a vital sorting out time for our memory bank. It is a well-researched fact that the memory plays tricks with us, like adding false memory to make sense of a partly remembered experience. These added memories are woven into the main theme and become part what we consider to be the truth. It's little wonder that the law courts have to work so hard to establish the truth!

When we recall our own experiences we need to be very conservative in our judgment and realize that our minds may not always record a completely true picture of an incident or event at which we were present. Try asking people leaving a political meeting to recall the main points that the speaker made, you will probably find, like I have, that there will be many different views expressed.

Bearing in mind, so to speak, some of the possible limits and fallibilities of our own brains and memories, let us journey into the next level of complexity, that of the mind itself.

THE MIND

IF THE BRAIN is the grey matter in our skulls, what is the mind? Brain and mind could be considered to be one and the same thing. However, I will assume that the mind is the functionality of the brain; a form of very advanced, parallel processing, computer software system. In reality, it is far more sophisticated than any known computer program simply controlling masses of data and memory. The mind can uncover novel and innovative thoughts, but unlike a computer, our minds can be subjected to uncontrollable thoughts, emotions and internal barriers.

I recall how, many years ago, I was called in to advise on a seemingly unsolvable problem at Reuters of Fleet Street. Aging technology was to be replaced by large mainframe computers. The company had a non-redundancy policy at the time. The problem was that they had a large work force of technicians servicing teleprinters; a technology based upon equipment introduced decades previously. It appeared that the technicians were unable to leap this substantial technology gap needed to maintain the computer systems. In attempting to re-train their staff they had reached a total impasse. However, after careful evaluation it transpired that the problem was not the complexity of the technology itself, but the technicians' perception of their own ability. Many of them had, as schoolchildren, been humiliated when they had been unable to grasp the fundamentals of fractions and algebraic equations, mathematics which was essential for understanding the new technology. Thus for reasons that they were too embarrassed to explain, they appeared to be overawed by the latest advanced technological systems.

It had been the negative thoughts based upon those long-ago and unhelpful experiences that had caused a mental barrier to be erected. Once the barrier was removed by empathy, care, encouragement and understanding, their progress was phenomenal. Within six weeks every one of them could, without exception, service and maintain the new technology. Their ability had been limited, not by their genetic inheritance, but by the active state of their emotional barriers.

Classical theory, beginning with Plato and Aristotle, points to a rationalist philosophy of emotions within the mind. These ideas have been modified and honed through centuries, perhaps receiving their fullest expression by Descartes in the seventeenth century, when he defined six primitive emotions: admiration, love, hate, desire, joy and sadness.

Today, using such things as MRI scans, there is much more emphasis on measuring direct relationships that may exist between brain and mind.

The cortex is where our thought processes are first seen to be happening in the brain. The action of the mind in the cortex then influences the lower brain/spinal chord - which in turn looks after the body's hormonal balance. These functions are subjected to quite large fluctuations due, in part, to our emotional state. Anticipation of danger, or even an important event in our personal world, ignites the "fight or flight" response, increasing the heart rate, blood pressure and breathing.

Our minds are influenced not only by external sights and sounds, but also by the many subtle chemical changes that take place within our brains, which in turn could be influenced by the state of our physical bodies. There are many internal and external phenomena that influence our thought processes such as; hyperthyroidism; endocrine gland secretions; chronic or acute disease processes; allergies to foods: moulds, vapors, and medications; seasonal affective disorder; hypnosis, meditation and the levels of dopamine and other chemicals in the brain itself.

With all this activity going on it is not surprising that the ability to control the tumbling thoughts of our own minds has always been seen as a problem for humanity. *The Bhagavad-Gita* speaks of the mind being very restless, turbulent, obstinate and very strong. Often depicted as four lively horses. The horses represent our false ego (pride), jealousy, greed (lust), and anger - all stirred up from what it terms "wrong thoughts".

On the other hand, there are examples from many places in the world where individuals excel in mind-control, or some would say mind-management. They range from a small number of Hindus who self mutilate their bodies, by embedding fearsome meat hooks in their own backs and parading in front of others, to Tibetan Buddhist monks who, in meditation, can sit overnight in temperatures well-below freezing with no apparent ill effects while being repeatedly covered by cold wet blankets. As well as the more obvious puzzle of pain suppression, the Buddhist practice appears to go beyond all known science to date, for reports suggest that the energy required to survive while also heating the blankets is much greater than that measured and recorded by their metabolic rate at the time.

Although there is much more to say about our computer-like minds that seem to be in control of all that we are, it is time to move on for there is still much of our journey to be traveled. The mind links strongly with consciousness so we will turn our attention to this higher level that heralds self-awareness.

CONSCIOUS THOUGHTS

TODAY MANY STILL use the ancient categories of the Vedantic scriptures that define the states of consciousness in broadly three ways: the state of deep (or dreamless) sleep, the waking state, and the dreaming state. They are all considered as illusionary. They further tell us that we are in fact part of the totality of things, part of an Ultimate Reality, to which we will all eventually return. Let us consider these things one at the time to see if any are relevant to our ultimate destiny.

Consider the state of being asleep and dreaming. Apparently we all need to dream; studies show that we normally dream for several hours every night - often dreams take just as long to enact as they would have done in the waking state.

When you are within the dream all is real. You are actually in a real city, being pursued by real monsters. You might feel the tingling sensations on your body as bloodsuckers suck out your life force. Within the dream there is no escape. You are intimately involved. When you are dreaming, it is as real as any other experience of life.

Think of the nightmare; even when one is fully awake it is not always easy to simply forget all about it. I recall many years ago, being abruptly woken from a peaceful slumber with a hard slap from my newly married wife because she had dreamed of some fanciful goings on between myself and a lady of ill repute!

Of course you can at times be aware, while still within the dream itself, that you are only dreaming, and struggle to wake up. Often you wake up, only to find that you are engaged in yet a further dream, which may continue for several layers of dream states, before you finally reach the awake state. This can be very alarming, especially if your first, apparent waking state, appears to be where you went to sleep, and all at first seems perfectly normal. I vividly remember the horror of such a sequence in an old Welsh farmhouse that we had brought back from the brink of extinction and had been living in for a few years. I was quite alone, and had fallen asleep by the log fire. I woke up stretched and got up out of the armchair intending to walk into the kitchen. To my horror I found that no matter how much I tried, I could not reach the kitchen. Then I woke up in the armchair again, and again and again. Had I visited another world, another reality? Whatever had happened, it was a very disconcerting reality!

When we are in the dream state itself, not only are things real, but we can also become aware that we are only asleep and know that when we do wake up, all will be well.

What about deep sleep, or dreamlessness? We do not have any recollection whatsoever of any thoughts, emotions or actions that we may well experience while we are in this state. It is from this mode, the mode of dreamless sleep, that ideas of perfect peace have been developed. It is suggested that perfection is nothing at all. No realization of anything. No feelings, thoughts, or joy. No disappointments. All is peace, even beyond the peace of the womb - perfect peace. To enter this perfect state, concepts such as having many lives, or being reincarnated through many lives, have been conceived. For the follower of the Upanishads, this perfect state is pure consciousness or liberation (a freedom and bliss which is beyond the temporary seven levels of heaven). For the Buddhist it would be Nirvana (a form of oneness yet nothingness).

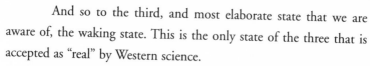

And so to the third, and most elaborate state that we are aware of, the waking state. This is the only state of the three that is accepted as "real" by Western science.

One could use the two sleep states (dreaming and dreamless) to explain the true meaning of this third state of our lives. If we assume that there is a pattern between all the states, then it is easy to see why, in Hindu and Buddhist philosophy, it is concluded that to be awake is simply another form of dreaming.

In some respects being awake is like the dream state. But the waking state has rules of its own. Our bank overdraft has the same value even after a good night's sleep! Things are tangible and real; they accumulate and continue, day in day out.

What we perceive, even in the waking state, is subject to distortion by the physical construction of our perceptual system such as in the Pulfrich illusion, where the sensory system acts as a highly selective filter. This filtering only allows some of the more important stimulation reaching the sensory receptors to reach consciousness, and is an essential part of our make up, for if we did not focus on a limited range of stimuli, we would be swamped with masses of unwanted, and irrelevant, information. Try driving a car in heavy, fast-moving traffic and "taking in" the detailed planting arrangements of all the gardens you pass by in an hour – on second thoughts it may be safer to simply look out through a stationary car window and realize that a few rain spots on the windscreen are conveniently ignored by the natural filtering process of our minds.

In practice we have many selective processes, which continually modify our understanding of the real world. The perception system not only selects information - it automatically organizes it into a coherent whole, and in so doing can time-shift reality to ensure an overall pattern with which it can cope.

Perception can do the work of inference, by searching for and obtaining information that directly verifies a causal interpretation. We automatically fill in information, when perception is inefficient or inadequate. It is a very strange world that our minds recall as true reality. What is represented in memory seems to be, to some extent, a non-literal representation of what was actually experienced.

The recall of an event depends on much more than the original event itself. Subsequent information, the effects of attitudes and values, the reactions of other people to the account, and even the level of arousal can alter the recall, and the representation in memory.

What we "see" is conditioned by our expectation and neural processing as well as the photons striking the retina.

Just as some people in sleep know they are dreaming, others seem to experience a deeper understanding of this earthly existence. Some, from their own experiences, agree with Eastern philosophy and conclude that the normal, or waking state could be considered another form of sleep, or illusion. It may be that if we transcend the limiting thoughts of simply being physical entities, we could become aware of a much higher state of consciousness and reality - a higher state that helps us to become more aware of our true purpose.

CONSCIOUSNESS

THIS IS WHERE the journey begins to move into the amazing territory of our own personal consciousness. In attempting to understand consciousness we are indebted to the immensely exciting and useful models derived by such great psychologists as Jung and Freud, and the very perceptive and valuable work of others such as Leibniz, who was convinced that God wished to create harmony between the individual and the materialistic world.

During my lifetime I have become more aware of my own consciousness. I have also investigated other people's findings about human consciousness. I have concluded that, as obvious as it may seem, the only consciousness that each of us experiences is our own. Hence, it is only our own consciousness that we are truly qualified to talk or write about.

It is our own, personal, consciousness that is most fully accessible to each one of us. The greatest psychiatrist or philosopher cannot improve his or her absolute knowledge of consciousness other than by observing him or herself. Models of consciousness should, ideally, be derived from an inner knowledge, and only be limited by the ability to express that knowledge. To try to observe other people's consciousness may be better than nothing, but it is filled with illusions, like looking into the distorting effects of a fairground's "hall of mirrors".

I intend to work towards the notion of an enlightened, transcendental, or *Grace-filled* consciousness; a consciousness that could perceive knowledge which may exist beyond the materialistic world

The basic processes of the brain and mind that we have encountered so far on our journey could be considered as the primary ones, where memories are forming and fading; logical thought takes place, and action can result. Observing this primary process is a secondary process, a consciousness. It is our consciousness that could well set us apart from other life forms.

There have been countless attempts to define consciousness. For our purposes we will consider an elementary, or first level consciousness as recognizing within ourselves that the following exists: our own physical bodies, the basic operations of our own minds, and the external world.

When this first level of consciousness is present, it is normally in the form of a strong ego, which often leads us to believe that we are in complete control of our destiny. We can even believe that we can selfishly ignore the wishes of others and do whatever we like, sometimes ignoring the consequences, sometimes relishing them. This is a state of mind that often attempts to suppress any caring emotions that might otherwise arise.

For most of us, this strong egocentric phase occurs in youth, and becomes less dominant as we pass into maturity. Unfortunately, everyone does not pass through their adolescent ego phase, and may even revert to their infantile emotions of non-empathetic desires and as a result, cause senseless destructive acts well into their adulthood.

However, I would like to consider how our own consciousnesses could change over our lifetime from being selfishly egocentric to becoming truly altruistic. One way of considering this development is to briefly examine how our priorities can change through our own personal and private internal dialogue. In particular

I would like to share some of my own *dialogue of comparisons* that have changed over my lifetime, and in so doing I hope that it will act as a trigger for you to consider your own personal and private internal conversations.

What is a *dialogue of comparisons?* At this first level of consciousness it is typically our awareness of our own body (and its preservation), our minds (and what we desire) and the rest of existence (including how we think of others).

To explore the ways in which we make conscious comparisons as we journey through life I will use three major comparisons that we inevitably make. These are firstly *my body* compared with *my mind* (or more precisely my very *being*), secondly *other people's needs* compared with *my own needs*, and finally *my truth* compared with *other people's truth*. In each of the cases below I would encourage you to sincerely consider some of your own thoughts, goals and agendas – by becoming the *me, my* and *I* for yourself in the following examples.

Consider **the first comparison**. How does my body relate to my very *being?*

Is there a difference between *me* and my body? For, after all, *me* is body, mind and consciousness. Yet I "look out"; I see my body mature, strengthen, dominate, age and then become weaker. It moves about, becomes affected by sun, rain, food and drugs. At times I become aware of a greater me, staring out from this body, at this body. The body can seem to have trapped me inside it.

I cannot escape its pain, its pleasure, its desire, its size, its shape and its physical place in the world. I am it. It is me. I am uniquely embedded within my body. It can become as oppressive as a tomb, or releasing and invigorating as I use it to express myself in dance, or rhythm, or sex, or laughter, or running across the barren windswept hills of my homeland. I cannot change my body, like I change my car. The pains, the pleasures are mine and mine alone. Consequently I turn to my consciousness and I ponder, or I pray, or I meditate and my body slowly becomes less important, as my understanding and experience of *being* broadens. For *being* seems to be of a different dimension. *Being* is the act of existence itself, which moves like a never-ending stream through the architecture of physical bodily life.

The second comparison is between other people's needs and *my* own needs. For me they range from selfishness, through puzzlement, to altruistic thoughts.

At one level I have felt that *I* am more important than others. In this case, the *I* includes my own mind, and embraces all my personal possessions and all that I can control, including other people. This is what I consider to be my primitive or animal state of being alive.

At times I find that I don't know what is more important really, other people's needs or my own. This has led my mind to wander in many directions. It could be the commencement of true compassion. However, my thoughts can degenerate into such thoughts as "Well, I will never know - nobody will ever know the true value of considering others", and this whole comparison loses interest. I do in effect "go to sleep" and drift through life's experiences at the level of a couch potato.

At other times I believe that other people's needs are more important than my own. This, perhaps, if acted out in everyday life for no personal gain whatsoever (not even any form of spiritual reward), is a truly altruistic characteristic, where altruism takes a form of selflessness beyond that which may be attributed to an evolutionary processes. In fact, it is a path that is at odds with self-survival. And when thoughts of God come to me they are perhaps a pointer to a deeper meaning for my life.

And so to **the third, and last comparison**. This is between what I consider to be true, compared with what others believe to be the truth:

Initially I believed that other people are the same as me, and have at least the same, and possibly more, understanding of consciousness and the meaning of life than myself. Gradually I realize the fallacy of this, for quite frankly, I don't know. I can only observe their outputs, their communication to me and the rest of the world. I cannot be sure of their true self, for they may be simply acting, and their ability to act could far exceed my own. In fact, other people's ability to pretend often seems superior to my own. I will never be fully sure anyway, for people are not constant. They change, sometimes temporarily, sometimes permanently. They experience an accident; inherit or lose vast amounts of money; grieve over the death of a friend or loved one; become disabled; live in the fog of depression; turn to drugs, or they may simply grow old and slowly fade away.

Finding other's truth depends, to a large extent, on my communication ability, mainly through language. Even though we share a common experience of sight and touch, language can seem to be inadequate to describe my reaction to the simplest objects in the real world, such as the emotions that can well up inside me by simply beholding a tree. I find that language to express internal emotions is boardering on the impossible, especially when I attempt to express my understanding of *being* and God. I may have developed a personal internal language that seems to embrace the transcendental, unfortunately when I externalize it, it takes on many shades of meaning, and I conclude that true transcendental communication occurs in silence.

I hope that the three comparisons, above, will help you to think through your own internal dialogue – for I believe that it is only through internal dialogue that we find the true path to an understanding of human consciousness. The comparisons hopefully help to clarify what I am calling the first level of consciousness. It is where we begin to become aware of our ability to choose, a sort of observation of our own mental processes. In many respects it is a primitive form of consciousness, and I suspect that it is existent, at least in part, in many life forms.

It is this first level of consciousness that many Western scientists and philosophers believe to be the full story. However, there is much more to consider, for we can keep climbing up and so become aware, even impartial observers of, this first level of consciousness.

CONSCIOUS AWARENESS

THE SOPHISTICATED PROCESS that we have been discussing, where we become aware of our own existence, is consciousness. But it is possible to even become aware of our own awareness. What I mean by that is that our elementary, or first order, consciousness can, itself, be observed by putting ourselves *outside* our first order consciousness. It is as if consciousness expands and becomes aware of itself. For me, it is as if a deeper understanding moves from the sub-consciousness, through consciousness towards *conscious awareness*, and I *know* that I have a full primary and secondary mental process, containing both mind and consciousness, within me, and that I am the observer of both.

Naturally, I cannot know if other people experience the same as myself, even if they are confronted with a similar set of conditions. Nevertheless, discussions with other people tell me that some people have a very deep level of conscious awareness, which can develop to become like a series of platforms, or layers, each observing the one below.

We could argue that there are infinite levels of consciousness, each one observing all the inner activity. This could account for the many ideas (which we will discuss later), concerning contemplation, meditation and prayer.

How can we distinguish between the first level of consciousness and the second level - the beginning of conscious awareness? Well, it is, to say the least, very difficult. When I discovered the great gift of knowing that *I am* and the profundity of *being*, it changed the way in which I perceived my whole world. Both my contentment and my excitement rose up in unison.

Whereas the first level is a form of monitoring and being aware of our desires, our own agenda, logic and organizational skills, conscious awareness implies an understanding of *being* itself.

As conscious awareness increases, the experience of *being* is automatically enhanced, for the two are bound together. As the levels of conscious awareness increases, so the mind moves from non-rational hopes and beliefs to a rational understanding of itself, then with humility and strength of purpose, it accepts the way the world actually is, while still attempting to create joy within that world.

With conscious awareness we surpass erotic, sexual love, and the instinctive bonding mothering love so prevalent in higher animals, primates and humans. We surpass the Greek *philos*, love and affection for our closest friends, and all forms of affection that stem from our biological self. We begin to glimpse true compassion, a compassion that is unattached and needs no personal reward whatsoever. As we ascend the levels, simple old Church hymns such as the one Anthony Pierce, the present Bishop of Swansea and Brecon, recently brought to my notice, take on a much fuller meaning, "My God, I love thee ... not for the sake of winning heaven, nor of escaping hell, not seeking a reward, (but) solely because thou art my God, and my most loving King." (*O blessed Jesus Christ*).

In this state of consciousness it is not important to us how people treat us, our friends or even our loved ones, we always reply with love and compassionate understanding. It is unfettered benevolence and goodwill of the highest good; it is the heart directing the mind. It does not expect love to be returned, and is most clearly shown in Jesus of Nazareth's dying words, when he says of his tormenters and killers, "Forgive them for they know not what they

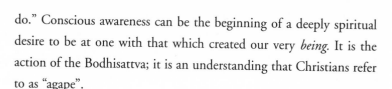

do." Conscious awareness can be the beginning of a deeply spiritual desire to be at one with that which created our very *being*. It is the action of the Bodhisattva; it is an understanding that Christians refer to as "agape".

Conscious awareness is enhanced and developed through the practice of contemplation, meditation and prayer.

We will know when we have a deeper experience of conscious awareness for we will automatically pass through a "singularity", like a tear of understanding, when all existence is viewed with compassion. This deeper experience is a state of Grace-filled, or transcendental consciousness. It is hard to hold onto at first, or in a crisis, and it takes much practice for it to be at the forefront of our consciousness. But Grace-filled consciousness unequivocally points us towards our goal in life. What then is Grace-filled, or transcendental consciousness?

GRACE-FILLED CONSCIOUSNESS

There are times when, quite suddenly, there will come into the consciousness a pulse of pure understanding. A pulse of pure overall awareness. A heartfelt cry. A peaceful acceptance in a sea of yearning. A teardrop of longing compassion for the very essence of all that is, was, and is to be. This is a *transcendental consciousness*, or what I term a *Grace-filled consciousness*. It is a state that can be experienced when sufficient conscious awareness, a critical mass so to speak, has accrued to form a mental singularity. It brings a realization that there is a oneness in all creation, and that *being* is existent and absolute.

Grace-filled consciousness and transcendental consciousness is, in many, if not all, respects, a similar mental state. Transcendental consciousness is experienced through the practice of deep meditation. Grace-filled consciousness is when the knowledge of God's presence fills the mind, for it is ultimately through the Grace of the Personal Creator, God, that this level of consciousness is achieved; although some belief systems fail to acknowledge the source of their transcendental state.

These ideas of inner awareness that we are considering are, for me, extremely difficult to describe. But once Grace-filled consciousness has been experienced, it will always be a part of one's make up, an inner voice of pure altruistic love.

I recall the Dalai Lama talking of a meeting with an old friend in Holland - their compassion for suffering humanity overwhelmed them to such an extent that, instead of a verbal greeting, they could only cry. There was simply nothing they could say to adequately to reflect their feelings. This is an example of a matured consciousness that has passed through the singularity of conscious awareness. It is so very different from the crying that is a reflection of our own personal suffering.

Many attempts have been made to express the depth of conscious awareness that heralds true altruistic compassion, Grace-filled consciousness. It is a state not bounded by science and, I believe, one that will never be subjected to the laws uncovered by scientific investigations. The eight-fold path in Buddhism, the seven levels of consciousness, the deepest message of love from the originators of great faiths such as Christianity and Sikhism, are but few of the many ways in which humanity has struggled to express the manifestation of this ultimate level of consciousness.

In reality Grace-filled consciousness is as an infinitely deep pool. It is in developing our conscious awareness that we eventually pass through a "singularity" and enter into the realm of transcendental consciousness, bringing both deep sorrow for other beings, and great joy for our own enlightenment. It is a pure, perfect tear of compassion.

Recognition of our spontaneous pulses of Grace-filled consciousness can take us through the experience of knowing our own *being*, into the true realization of God, and on to an understanding of the ultimate purpose for our existence. Whether you consider Grace-filled consciousness and transcendental consciousness to be the same or a different experience there is no doubt that both are completely and unequivocally altruistic. They are not concerned with any aspects of self-survival or self-gratification, and can only be achieved when our inner mind becomes humble and associates with other people's joys and sorrows. They are beyond family and other loyalties, giving empathy and love for existence itself, and in the case of Grace-fill consciousness realizing a connection with the creator of that existence. Its realization is the greatest gift given to us by the Grace of God. It is the Christian ideal. It is the goal of the journey to Buddhist enlightenment. It is an inner light that cuts through the darkest of nights.

Transcendental, Grace-filled consciousness is boundless; it excels *all* possible depths of academic knowledge and understanding. It will never be logically deduced or scientifically measured, but will only be understood through personal experience. When pulses of understanding at the transcendental level become continuous, we begin to live in the presence of God. But before we investigate the actual methods of developing and managing our minds it is important to decide just how all these things affect our daily lives. Do our day-to-day experiences allow us to expand our consciousness to encompass its full potential? We may well be able to measure the brain's activity with science, probe the mysteries of the mind with advanced psychology and cognitive techniques, but we will only begin to truly understand the realms of the consciousness by reflecting on our own experiences.

We need to integrate our understanding of consciousness with the world around us, if we are to progress and to reach our goal of knowing the purpose of our existence.

CHAPTER 4

THE LAND OF PEOPLE

THE EVERYDAY

HAVING EXPLORED SOME of the concepts of the brain, mind and consciousness, we are still left with the fact that our emotional state can change the way we perceive the world around us. Perception of reality may also be distorted by a thumping headache, just as wax in the ear can distort sounds. This means that when we observe other people's behavior we have to try and allow for our own imperfections, and realize that often it is not reality that we are experiencing but simply the way in which our bodies and minds react to our everyday experiences.

As well as our own imperfections and mood changes, other people we meet are not constant emotionless objects but subject to many external and internal changes themselves. One day they may feel a great sense of well-being, but by the next day an experience may have happened to them which changes their whole outlook on life.

And so to the land of people.

If God has decreed that we are all intrinsically equal, then it seems surprising that equality is not reflected in our everyday world.

We are not players on a level playing field. People are born male or female, tall or short, physically able or suffering a range of disabilities. Our genetically transmitted talents for art, music, love, and logic are developed through our varying and unequal experiences. We start life in a particular social culture, a given class, a creed, a race and in a part of the world that may be in abject poverty or filled with golden opportunities. We could be a smiling Down's Syndrome child or develop to become another Beethoven. Our bodies could mature so that we become the fastest runner on earth. We could be born blind or profoundly deaf. We could be gripped by undesirable addictions, lose our self-control, develop bi-polar disorder or we could bathe in the continuous calmness of inner peace. Our freedom of choice can be diminished by disease, enslavement, natural disaster or even by prejudice.

Life all too often seems to be unfathomable, finding suffering where there should be joy, and joy where we would expect to find only suffering. However, as we are seeking an underlying purpose to life we cannot simply ignore the suffering and inequalities all around us, for I have a hunch that it has developed as God intended. To become a recluse in a monastery may calm our agitated minds and allow us a glimpse of peace, but would we see the full reflection of God's purpose if we suppress our emotions and ignore the common events of life? There could well be profound pointers to the meaning of our lives embedded within the multiplicity of the ordinary. If there are, then it is up to us to discover just what they are, and what they imply.

To demonstrate, and hopefully clarify, what I mean I will share with you some of my own experiences. These experiences form a set of case studies, intended to act as catalysts for you to think through similar experiences of your own. For I believe that through reacting to our own experiences and then pondering on them we will not only find clues for the meaning of life, but we may also be able to free our minds, from everyday distractions, for the journey to come.

I have chosen three cases to illustrate four stages of humanity, paralleling the Hindu, or some would say the Shakespearian, stages that we go through as we mature. They are "the basic instincts of childhood", "the influences of youth" and "adulthood and the onset of wisdom".

The ability to manage our own thoughts is very difficult, for as we have discussed, our minds are very subtle and crafty and can be likened to four lively horses: angry, proud, greedy and jealous.

The first case study concerns childish anger. From the moment we take our first breath, to the moment of death, we so easily revert to selfishness and become aggressive.

BASIC INSTINCTS

THE FIRST TIME I can recall being aggressive was when I was four years old. The Second World War was at its height. I had spent the previous twelve months in a British hospital at Pontypool during which time my parents had become like strangers to me. It happened on my return home.

My mother had been very busy in our terraced cottage in the village of Griffithstown. She had arranged the spartan kitchen especially for my homecoming. A large wooden table was centre stage, practically filling the tiny room. Its glowing white boards had been scrubbed so often that the darker annual rings stood proud, a series of parallel tracks that later reminded me of the railway marshalling yards where my father worked.

I was put to sit in a high chair, which gave me my first feeling of being uncomfortable. Surely I was not going to be treated as a baby!

My shyly smiling mother had prepared the dinner. My agitation increased. I began to feel quite deprived. Where were my friends, the pretty nurses and the large open space of the hospital rooms that I had become so familiar with?

When my mother finally put my dinner in front of me, my agitation burst into anger.

Glaring at my father's plate, I shouted, "It's smaller than his!"

I picked up my own plate and threw it across the room.

"This place is horrible. I want to go home!"

The dinner landed on the wall and I somberly watched the potato and gravy sliding down its whitewashed surface.

My mother burst into tears. Thankfully, my father said nothing. I cannot remember if my sister, Joan, was there or not.

There were only the sobs of my mother breaking the stillness.

I began to feel perplexed. Then quiet. Then sorry. Then humbled. And finally guilty at hurting this kind lady.

Even at such a young age it seems that tears can give us a different level of understanding and help us to be aware of other people's emotions. I feel sure that if my father had, through his own frustrations, become angry with me, I would not have felt that inner kindness which seemed to well up from deep within me.

And to this day I still am aware that I have both love and anger, like the weave and weft of the fabric of my personality; although as I grow older I am thankful that my anger is much harder to ignite than my love.

On Monday 24th March 2003 an article by Melanie Phillips of the *Daily Mail* illustrated for me how righteous anger can be fuelled. Her article concerned the 2003 Iraqi war. She wrote, "According to Kenneth Joseph, a young American pastor whose trip to Iraq as a human shield 'shocked me back to reality', the Iraqis convinced him that Saddam was 'a monster the likes of which the world had not seen since Stalin and Hitler. Their tales of slow torture and killing made me ill, such as people being put into a huge shredder for plastic products, feet first so all could hear their screams as bodies got chewed up from foot to head'."

Such reporting made the case for war in Iraq very real. History is littered with instances of war as a solution. People of integrity have argued that *war* would herald more suffering and increase world conflict. To others, who sincerely believe in *just* wars, lack of conflict would, in the long run, increase world tension and lead to even more suffering. Both parties are convinced that they are putting forward rational arguments based upon moral principles. But all too often there is insufficient information, which is then fuelled by presuppositions, subjectivity, emotion, and hidden agendas aimed at securing material or political gains. Then there are even religious, or more correctly, political fanatics who advocated that God condones killing.

I cannot imagine God reacting to war with such enthusiasm; the only human emotions that I could anticipate God taking on would be those of despair and compassion.

There are many dichotomies concerning war even in our world scriptures. In the New Testament gospels we have, "Blessed are the peace makers", but such sentiments are tempered with violence in other parts of the gospels where it is said that that even peacemakers have to, on times, use force. Certainly Arjuna's momentous and ethical battle for God, but against his own family, as recorded in the Hindu Bhagavad-Gita, illustrates the terrible dilemma of war.

And when I reflect on my own state of mind, especially as a child returning home from that wartime hospital, I realize that much aggression can start with quite simple perceived provocation, and if circumstances permit, could escalate into killing and war.

So it seems to me that although I am far from an advocate of war, at times we can only prevent injustice by the use of an overwhelming force. As long as the sabre-tooth tiger roams free within the very mind of man, we will always need brave and courageous people to protect the innocent, the needy and the feeble. Perhaps this implies that the best protection is the sword of righteousness welded with a delicate hand, for it can be impossible to negotiate with murderers and fanatics who have nothing to lose and are bound within their own desires. Are all wars evil, or could they be like a ring of cleansing fire that burns away the old bracken to allow green shoots to grow anew?

To work through such difficult questions I can only return to my own experience. I find that if I am threatened, while outwardly I may be forced to conform, my inner mind can "dig its heels in", waiting for the threat to disappear before reverting to my old ways. If, on the other hand, I am moved by compassion my mind is changed, often permanently. Throughout my life my father's anger, non-violent as it was, changed me little (except to do the opposite of his will if a chance arose!). My mother's tears over my own wrongdoings have stayed with me for life. Could compassion form the basis of our future response to other people's aggression, a way of breaking the cycle of vengeance, which is no more than a form of tit-for-tat anger?

I believe this could be where we differ from animals in that although we respond to force and fear, we also have the ability to respond even more to love and compassion. Harper Lee in his book *To Kill a Mockingbird* suggests that empathy could become so strong that it is like climbing into someone's skin and walking around in it".

We will only win hearts and minds when we walk around in others skins, learn to understand their needs and to share what we have. I believe that any permanent victory will not be achieved by force, but by the more lasting weapon of love, perhaps tempered with compassionate containment for the few.

Aggression may have helped our evolution, but it will not lead us to the next level of human complexity or a worthwhile individual destiny.

THE INFLUENCES OF YOUTH

SPUD HOLDER FELT that he was the philosopher of our teenage gang of nine boys - the well-read member of the group; bespectacled, red flat hair and still wobbling within his remaining puppy fat.

We were sitting with our bums carefully resting on the convenient, mud-colored, wooden window ledge of the town's master draper, when Spud waxed eloquent about his latest revelation.

"If we aren't careful, Mike, all the nice girls will be gone and we will be left with the dregs!" He stopped, waiting for this great philosophical outpouring to overwhelm me.

"S'pose so." I muttered.

"The good ones will all be gone soon." He was obviously trying his best to alarm me.

"S'pose so." I repeated.

Later, on the way home, my energetic stride became ponderous. My new-grown body, which normally dominated my thinking when walking through the streets, seemed to shrink into insignificance as I concentrated on Spud's words. The more I visualized the attractive local girls of seventeen, the more I realized that they seemed to be fading; melting like snow in the early spring sun.

Yes, he could be right, they could soon be gone. All the girls of our age were being snapped up by male predators who were a few years older.

Before I arrived home I had become convinced that he was right.

I became alarmed, for in those far off days in the nineteen-fifties I knew that a person could end up for an entire lifetime with someone that they did not like, let alone love.

The coming months became, for me, a fervor of activity as I threw myself into the frantic turmoil of the local dances. Dating one girl after another, rejecting for looks, for an odd comment, for an improper suggestion. Or sometimes being rejected myself, often for staying with my mates too long in the pub.

I certainly took Spud's words to heart. What if he had said, "Your country needs you to fight", or "Jesus needs you." Would I have become a trained killer, or an evangelist?

Although I believe we have freewill, it is not easy to be sure just how much of our life is predestined by cause and effect, or preordained by God.

The issue of predestination again became uppermost in my mind a few years ago when I had the good fortune to accompany Bishop Dewi for a day, during his sponsored one hundred and twenty mile walk from one end of what was then his diocese of Swansea and Brecon, to the other. He told me that he had decided to join the ministry of the church when he was seven years' old. Not from any sudden revelation, or classroom learning, but through the simple evolution of his character, and the local dynamic Christian environment into which he had been born. His Nonconformist mother and Anglican father soon had Dewi in the church choir. His aspiration, along with the continual backing of his observant parents, meant there was never a thought of any other career.

I have often noticed that things seem to evolve and change imperceptibly slowly. For example, I know that, way back, my mother believed that God had placed everyone in a certain family, under certain conditions and there was no way of changing that fact. "The rich man in his castle, the poor man at his gate", was more than just a hymn to her. In those early years she felt that we were completely conditioned by the circumstances of our birth. But she changed, for when my wife-to-be first met my mother, my mother had already become middle class. By the time she had reached her late eighties she had evolved into a person proud of her "noble" birth.

Chance then, so it seems, has a lot to do with who we are and how we view the world. We all appear to be part of a great game of chance involving our social background, physical prowess, mental gifts and what we just happen upon as we go through life. It should come as no surprise that so many people conclude that the human condition is nothing more than a series of random chances. This could be because they believe that all meaningful goals are confined to a physical world and human values. Perhaps they become so mesmerized by worldly things and what others may think of them that they are afraid to truly open up their minds to the possibilities beyond the phenomenal. Yet the truth is that we can influence "who we become" in many ways, and in so doing substantially effect our ultimate destiny.

ADULTHOOD AND THE ONSET OF WISDOM

THIS LAST CASE study introduces many of the emotional turmoils and ethical conundrums that we all face in our daily lives. Conundrums that we have to face up to if we are to glimpse God's purpose and in so doing perhaps realize our own ultimate purpose. The case study concerns a very simple incident, yet it embraced many things as it slowly moved me to prayer.

One of the biggest mysteries has been for me, "How can a loving and compassionate God allow suffering?" This case is not about the suffering of the born poor, the exploited, the victims of massive tsunamis or even the sick and disabled, but with the suffering we come across within an affluent society.

I invite you to step along with me through the thin veil of "sanity" as we are all prone to do at some point in our lives, into a state of existence that any one of us whether rich or poor, clever or dull, worldly or shy, could become overnight. Much depends upon our own ability to conform to social norms and to manage our own minds. The terrible truth is that one in four of us will, at some time in our lives, suffer mental illness! So join me and see where even a simple act, like having a cup of tea, can lead.

It was 7.30 pm the night before bonfire night when I walked into the brightly lit warmth of Kesgrave's new Tesco Supermarket cafeteria and found that drinks and cakes were still being served. After a tiring journey from Wales to the east coast of England, I decided to really indulge. Selecting a large piece of passion cake, I added a pot of tea and extra water. This was to be my glimpse of heaven. As no one knew me, I could completely relax and allow my mind to indulge itself in its own freewheeling thoughts.

Having just paid the relatively insignificant sum for this 'glimpse of heaven', I started to meticulously select some suitable cutlery for my indulgence, reflecting how, in the past, even consuming the most sumptuous meal at London's Dorchester Hotel, my satisfaction had been no better than it was now.

A sudden chill came over me. What if I had not even possessed the small sum of money to pay for the cake and tea? How could I survive? I was so very blessed to be able to simply enjoy all this for so little effort. Yes, so very blessed indeed.

I absent-mindedly gazed around the almost deserted, clinical tables and chairs. There was only a couple of staff talking earnestly in the far corner.

Then my eyes fell on a most hideous and frightening sight.

Just beyond my right elbow was a gaunt, battered face of what appeared to be an eighteenth-century prizefighter. His laser eyes sent their beams into my very being. The streaky grey and black unshaven mask-like face was scarred and battered from receiving heavy blows, causing his right eyebrow to be distorted and bloated in a bloody mess, his strong triangular nose covered with the deep red of yet unscarred tissue. His hard-set jaw and his mouth of steel signaled envy and hate. The gaunt face was so compelling that I became momentarily mesmerized by its overall whiteness. The face, a terrifying white mask, suspended in mid-air by invisible forces, sent a shiver down my spine.

It took all my concentration to look away from, and walk past that terrible sight. As I approached a suitable table, a voice followed me, and caught hold of me.

It was from the White Face! My heart started pounding. I had to concentrate really hard to decipher the words. To my relief the sentence became, "What's the weather like outside now then?"

The harsh real world outside had now forgotten the longest, hottest summer on record. Icy winter blasts were everywhere.

"Very cold. Could be a hoar frost later." I started mechanically pouring tea to regain my meditative posture. Better not even look at him, for fear of becoming a target for his aggression. (I'd witnessed it all long ago in the dance halls, "What are you staring at me for?" Then wham, without warning, the first fist would make contact.)

He faded from my thoughts as I glanced through the girlie photographs in the paper with its taunting messages of how cruel or how sexy some people had been, peppered with contrary statements of how we should not propagate such degenerate ideas.

My analysis was interrupted by a voice from the White Face. I casually looked towards it. A pretty little waitress was standing by his table. I felt the tension rise within me, and I became acutely aware of the exact position of everything around. At the same time I was deeply conscious of my inadequacy if the situation took a turn for the worse. I would be no match for this hardened man. I visualized a body of steel hidden beneath his dirty and torn clothing. Then I noticed that his trousers were spattered with a light red.

Blood?

The thought that he could even have killed someone that night slammed into me. To my relief the young waitress seemed not to notice anything unusual, and cheerfully moved to his bidding, clearing away the torn paper that he had piled high on the ashtray, causing it to spill over the edge.

The face gained height - floating on top of an ominous, six-foot body.

He was now standing with his back to me by the tea-making machine. He had been around, he knew all about survival in the urban jungle. His shoes were practically non-existent - over half of each sole had been completely worn away.

He turned so quickly that I did not have time to avert those penetrating eyes.

"You're frum Wales," he growled. He walked towards his table, and as he was putting his tray down, I heard an unfamiliar, high pitched voice which must have been my own, "Of course, where else?"

"I'm frum Mountain Ash, my father worked in the Big Dowlas Pit."

Quite suddenly his ringing voice had become clear, almost friendly, as he mentioned Mountain Ash, a South Wales Valley town that had, like him, been ravaged by the past. He walked towards my table and held out his hand, and when it covered mine it took on the properties of a vice.

My fear began to melt. If we were only to have a war of words, I was confident of my own survival. My concern now shifted onto the sad state of this fellow human being. He began to appear more like a man utterly beaten by society. His physical strength had kept him alive but to improve, to interact in society as it now presented itself to him, was beyond his control.

"Come and sit down and join me if you like," I ventured. He talked on, still standing, his big hand resting his weight on my table, a hand which was covered with psoriasis in a chronic stage, the untended sores disappearing up past his wrist into the ripped and filthy anorak; an anorak several sizes too small.

"Bring your tea over here," I again requested. Now he was in full flood, nothing would stop his torrent of words; words which he lavishly punctured with "Taff", which I presumed he hoped I would understand as a Welsh brotherhood. He transferred his tray to my table.

I interrupted his flow to announce, "My name is Michael." By descending a few octaves and rising a few decibels, my voice had finally returned to normal. His hand found mine; again the vice-like grip and vigorous shaking.

"Michael, and my name is Barry, as in Barry Island," assuming that I had intimate knowledge of the fairgrounds and sands of that South Wales seaside town. Now he started talking in earnest, an unstoppable monologue. His voice lowered. He tried to hunch forward to increase the intimacy, but his square shoulders and straight back only seemed to allow him to bend from the waist!

"I've bin in jail for 20 years! ... Only got out in June. ... Things are very tough ... My mother died when I was fourteen ... Come down from Norwich today ... Where's the town around 'ere ... Any more shops around 'ere?"

I interjected comments at the appropriate moments. When I asked why he had been in jail that long he simply scowled.

Then came the inevitable punch line, "Gor any money on you?"

"Yes, about three pounds."

"Can you see your way clear to giving me a cuttle u pounds?"

"I might. I'll have to think about it."

With that he launched into an attack on the local clergy who apparently just wanted to get him into bed! The uncaring police who had just beaten him up! And the fact that even the soup kitchens set up by the Salvation Army only let you have a meal for one day and you could never return to them. He had an overwhelming urge to go to the town that night; could I drive him or at least give him money for the bus? All this, and much more, punctured with lavish supplies of, "Taff."

On impulse, I offered him the shoes that I was wearing, unfortunately my size tens were too small. I offered him my own, fairly new coat. He put this on with relish over his existing garments, and zipped it up with gusto. At last the white face began to melt into a slight smile.

"Can't give me a cuttle u pounds as well now can you?" He had refused a meal earlier, so I simply repeated, for about the tenth time, "You will only spend it on drink, so there is no point."

"No I wont, Taff, honest, I won't." Came the now familiar reply, wringing with sincerity.

So, I added, "Can't manage both the coat and the three pounds. I will have to get another one, only this time it will have to be from Oxfam." I was hoping that he would take the coat. But no, he triumphantly took off the coat, his face breaking into a broad grin as he raised his voice for the entire world to hear his proclamation,

"I'll sell, you this coat, Taff, for three pounds! Yes, you can buy it off me for three pounds, and that's a bargain, Taff!" I was utterly disappointed. What hope had this poor wretch! He may survive for a while. He had murdered someone when he had found his wife in bed with the neighbor. He was forty-seven years old. He had no future - only a past. No home, no innate or learned ability to plan his future.

Was I going to be, like so many before me, about to give him a token just so that he would go away? To find someone else. To leave my life intact. To simply pay him off. I tried to console myself; after all he was a useless member of society. Even so my mind somehow would not seem to accept …

As I silently handed over the money. We both knew so much. We said nothing.

I had nothing to add.

Then he spoke, quietly, almost a whisper, words which completely humbled me,

"Pray for me … Please pray for me, Taff."

Words that seemed to well up from the depths of his very soul. The eyes were now the softness of warm, deep pools.

I rose, murmuring that I would and, putting on my coat, walked silently away.

An evening that had started with my anticipation of a simple indulgence had turned into a somber reminder of the utter helplessness of so many of our fellow beings.

In the span of some thirty or forty minutes I had experienced so much – fluttering of greed, fear of being penniless, simple lust, afraid of being physically hurt, indifference, hypocrisy, concern for the innocent, feelings of superiority, unexpected understanding and empathy, inquisitiveness and intense awareness, compassion, humility and despair. Through all that emotional turmoil I now believe that I had acquired a little spiritual development, and perhaps even a modicum of wisdom.

I now realize that I will never discern the meaning of someone else's life. There is no real means of knowing Barry's degree of consciousness, his joy or his suffering. We are not Barry, and in the end we can only accept the fact that we have a chance to develop ourselves by acting with the understanding that we have come to know. We can feel compassion and care for all who are beset by pain, worry, anxiety, depression, and suffering whatever the cause. And we can pray that we become sufficiently developed in ourselves so that we may take a little of their suffering from them.

Maybe it's in our struggle to understand that helps our Conscious Awareness to develop, and through this development we are given pointers to the reason for our lives. For we are like strangers in a foreign land, unable to fathom why the ultimate power of the land allows things to be as they are. But, it is God's creation. It is God's world. We are products of God's will and if we wish to continue our journey of discovery we will have to look with freshness at the wisdom of the sacred words of those who have gone before us, and try to distil their true essence.

PART III

RELIGION

CHAPTER 5

THE LAND OF RELIGION

THE ESSENCE

THE "LAND OF RELIGION" is massive, with millions of individuals, groups, sects and mainstream organizations, some of whom feel that they have a monopoly of the truth. With such a plethora of faiths I have come to realize that all aspects of religion, faith, meditation and prayer have to be approached with an open yet discerning mind for, as well as the tremendous insight to be gained from some, there are also many false prophets waiting to lead us away from the timeless wisdom to be found in religious teaching.

For me the word "religion" includes all forms of shamanism and earth- based beliefs, as well as Zoroastrian, Jewish, Christian, Islamic, Hindu, Buddhist, Tao, Confucius and Shinto based religions, along with belief systems such as Darwinism and Humanism. In fact anything that stands or falls on a belief rather than a proof, that can be scientifically demonstrated, is a form of religion.

Although the vast majority of all belief systems intrinsically reach for truth, do they all achieve it? Are some faiths doomed to lead us into an impenetrable forest, an uncrossable crevasse, or a pointless cul-de-sac? These are difficult and often emotive questions, which are not easy to answer.

We could take the formal path and find out about the founders, the history, meaning, interpretation, worship, rituals, practice and laws of the classical world religions and their many subgroups. For this approach the best place to start is *The Encyclopaedia of Religion*. However, our journey is to be an excursion into the very essence of religious teaching, to bypass the academic in an attempt to glean the timeless truths which are to be found at the heart of so many of our great world religious movements. Yet we cannot completely bypass the world around us, for all religions and faith systems are firmly anchored on the phenomenal, or worldly plane. This means that they normally support a hierarchical structure, have developed practices and expect allegiance to their own brand of ethics. Due to their need for an organization base, and the fact that even the simplest religious person needs means of support, they become involved in some form of wealth creation which ranges from a begging bowl to multinational commercial activities.

And when we observe and analyze other's experience and action we are confronted with what seems to be a Herculean task. On the one hand there are the self-centered, ego-driven individuals, humility playing little part in their private internal dialogue. They observe the world with an inner, smug smile. On the other hand there are those who are predominantly altruistic, realize *being*, care for other's welfare, for their unhappiness and stress, and often shed a silent tear for them. Whereas the latter often feel the pain of others, the ego-driven become hardened and, if circumstances allow, can even become brutal.

Unfortunately, to the observer both the ego-driven and the altruistically-driven may appear to be sensitive and caring - but for the former it is a play to impress themselves, other people and even God! While for the latter the suffering of others is a truly painful experience. Sadly, on top of these difficulties there are some individuals, under the umbrella of religion, who decide that they occupy a special place in the cosmos and succumb to personal ambition, politics, and selfish greed. Such people tear the heart out of all religious ideals.

Although there is much to learn from others, in the end the only way that we can find out about our ultimate destiny, as I am sure you will agree, is by *putting ourselves in the experiment*, so to speak, and attempting to develop our Consciousness Awareness, until we begin to permanently live in an enlightened state or as some would say, in the presence of our Personal Creator, God.

It is our minds that have to be made ready. They have to become filter, rejecting the surface noise and bustle of the world and much of traditional religious practice, until we become aware of an inner truth, that awesome, timeless resonance. To achieve this state of awareness, the human race has developed many procedures over thousands of years, which have to be integrated with our daily emotions and experiences. These procedures require us to have a purposeful sequence to our thoughts. We have to become observers of our world and, more importantly, of our own thoughts, until our consciousness is able to recognize the signals of destiny.

And amazingly such knowledge is within the grasp of us all. It started for me at a very young age, as it does for us all. I can still hear adults saying, "You can't keep your cake and eat it", which I interpreted as, I couldn't keep my pocket money (in the nineteen forties this included my government issued stamps in a Ration Book!) and have sweets. After all this time I still struggle with my simple day-to-day choices. For example, I enjoy eating biscuits and my instinct is to eat all I can. But, fortunately I usually enter into discussion with myself. I reason that it is unhealthy to eat so many high fat, sugar-based products at one time. I can then either ignore the second "voice" or I can allow it to lead my thoughts. In taking the latter course of action, my resolve to be healthy is re-enforced.

This simple example illustrates the beginning of mind control. It is only through the control of, or more correctly - the management of, our own minds that we will become conscious of our inner divine spark and the wisdom of grace. To develop this inner focusing of our minds, meditation, prayer, scripture and talking to people of faith are tools we can call upon, tools with which we can hone our thoughts and so begin to influence our ultimate destiny.

The next stage of our journey is about opening our minds and letting our tumbling thoughts go, leaving all fear, resentment and anger behind and allowing, ourselves to be washed with layers of understanding. An understanding of a truth, which, in the end, we will find is beyond all language and ritual.

MEDITATION

IN MID-DECEMBER 1991 I was sitting cross-legged on a thickly carpeted floor, listening to a reading of the Sikh Holy Scripture, the *Sri Guru Granth Sahib ji*.

This particular reading was to be the complete 1,430 pages and would take forty-eight hours of continuous reading. The occasion was to commemorate the Ninth Guru's birthday, Sri Guru Teg Bahadur ji. Over three hundred years' ago, he was asked to act as a spokesman for faiths that were being suppressed. Of his own free will, he went to the Islamic Emperor to plead the case for free worship, only to be eventually beheaded because he would not deny his convictions.

The floor of the Sikh Gurdwara was as welcoming as ever as I sat in humble meditation. Suddenly a pair of naked feet appeared before me, and a voice sounded from above, speaking I knew not what. Awakened, I opened my hands to receive the blessing of the butter-rich Prasad from an elderly Indian lady. She would have offered the Prasad in the same way if I had been a tramp or a king.

In the quiet hours that followed, surrounded by the protective meditations of others, my own meditations revealed to me deep universal relationships. My cluttered mind moved freely in its associations and my thoughts gently traveled along the path of understanding more of life and its awesome opportunity. An opportunity to know more, to love more, and to give more to that benevolence that allowed me to exist in the first place.

What was this meditation that I was experiencing? Was it more than the contemplation experienced when sitting quietly in the natural world? Was it more than the deep appreciation that my mind experiences when it mingles with poetry or fine music? Was it more than being dumbstruck by the sheer awesomeness of being conscious of my own existence in a cosmos where the number of stars in the sky is a million times more than all the grains of sand on earth, and I was like a recursive dot, on a dot, on a dot ... ?

It was all these things and much, much more ...

And I can only recommend that you try such an experience for yourself, in a gurdwara, church, mosque, temple, synagogue or simply by choosing a quiet place in the natural world; perhaps using one of the first five meditations outlined later on in this chapter.

There are within the boundaries of our minds, a whole host of latent programs waiting to be called upon and developed. To access these deeper programs many systems have been developed. For example there is the *t'ai chi* breath and movement of Taoism, the visualisation of shamanism, the re-living contemplation from the life of Christ recommended by Saint Ignatius of Loyola.

Although forms of meditation have found their expression from time immemorial and are present to some degree in all cultures, the most rational grouping is to be found in the ancient Hindu philosophies, where these meditations are referred to as a form of yoga. Of these, perhaps seven have been most written about and practiced.

These seven most commonly recognized meditative practices have a vast school of philosophy and practice behind each one. All can induce a sense of inner peace and tranquility, giving us an escape from the ebb and flow of our physical world. Although many religious movements claim that the experiences of meditation are unique to their form of belief, in reality, meditation in some form is universal.

The seven are briefly:

First there is a practice that centers on observation of one's own breathing. Many groups use it as an introduction to meditation. Eastern practitioners know it as Hatha yoga, which goes much further than the relaxing techniques of the West. It involves purification and discipline of the physical body, along with postures and diet, and is used to calm the mind and body. It is thought to increase the bodily supply of invisible life energy, *prana*, that permeates the universe.

Second there is bringing the mind to "one-pointedness", sometimes called Dhyana yoga, a popular form of meditation with some Buddhist practitioners. This is a way to remember the eternal by contemplating a visual form representing a cosmic reality. It is part of most religious practice. For example the focus may be on an icon, a candle flame, a crucifix, a picture, sacred writings, a blank wall, or a part of nature itself such as a pebble or a bubbling spring of water. During meditation the clear light of awareness can allow insights to arise spontaneously, which, according to some, include colored lights or even visits from immortal beings. The ultimate goal is a super-conscious state of union with "That which allowed us all to be". The state and the experience vary according to the underlying belief of the meditator.

Third is where energies are believed to be exchanged between the body and the outer environment. This is the practice of Kundalini yoga. It is the practice of opening the subtle energy centers (chakras). There are seven major centers, located on the vertical axis of the body, starting from the base of the spine and finishing at the most refined of the chakras, which is located in the brain, the seat of cosmic consciousness.

Practitioners of complementary medicine under the heading "Relaxation and Visualisation techniques" are increasingly using these first three forms of meditation in the West. They include being aware of all that is going on around you, while being in the meditative state. Observation of the breath is the most common Western adaptation, along with such practice as:

The candle technique – contemplating, with unblinking eyes, a lighted candle until the eyes water, then closing eyes and seeing a little flame in the "third eye", at the centre of the forehead; if it slips to the side you "bring it back" to the centre.

Pulling the healing energy - a form of visualization for spiritual healing.

The aim is to pull healing energy through the body by concentrated imagination. For example, imagining good cells facing and overpowering the bad cells in the body.

Fourth is the well-known technique of bringing peace, and a feeling of well-being, by the repetition of certain words, or sounds, known as Mantras. For Christians the word could be "Jesus" while for the Hindu it could be "OM", or "AUM", and so forth. Chanting the mantra allows the consciousness to ride over the sea of the mind, raising the natural vibration of the meditator, who becomes more and more attuned to the Divine Ground of Existence. A Mantra is a tool for stilling the restless mind, by giving it something to hold on to. Transcendental Meditation (TM) has popularized this form of meditation. It is being increasingly used in modern worship song in many parts of the world.

Fifth is perhaps my favorite way of introducing meditation, for I believe that it naturally takes one more step than the first four. It is the way of wisdom, the mind seeking the inner self. It is a form of meditation known as Jnana yoga. The seeker develops spiritual virtues of calmness, restraint, renunciation, resignation, concentration and faith, then finds the Self within by self–interrogation, such as asking "who am I" and finally realizing the Self through the ultimate wisdom of spiritual insight, rather than intellectual knowledge. It is a way to realize *being*, an absolute truth, and clearly points to the existence of God. This is more fully explored in my book *Beyond All Reasonable Doubt*.

The last two, below, are best practiced after God has been realized in the mind (God as always in this book stands for that which is beyond the phenomenal world. The word God is not intended to be associated with any particular belief system).

Sixth is the way of love, a Bhakti meditation. There are three basic approaches to Bhakti. The first is where there is no outward display of the love of God. The worship is private. It can be monastic. The second approach is by the person who, wearing best clothes, attends a communal place of worship to God, in social fellowship. And the third type, who practice the way of love, are those who are so elated in their love of God that they shout it from the rooftops, the charismatics.

Seventh and last is the form of meditation known as Karma yoga, the way of work. Karma yoga is to be found in many religions. For example Brother Lawrence (c. 1605-91, a Carmelite lay brother of the Christian faith) practiced quieting his mind so that he would be in communion with God as he carried out his menial chores in a noisy, bustling monastic kitchen. He worked, "For the love of God".

Saint Paul in the New Testament advocates that, along with God's grace, our good actions have little value if our reason for doing those actions is not pure.

Karma meditative practice is the way of unattached work. It requires us to be fully involved in the real world of action, and not to be affected by what the world gives back to us. Expect no reward whatsoever, not even a "thank you", and then any ingratitude will not harm you, because you never expected anything.

One of the best books I have ever read on the practice of this form of yoga, *Karma-Yoga* written by a very intellectual and spiritual Hindu Swami, Vivekananda who made his mark on history in 1898 at the first World Parliament of Religions in Chicago. His teaching is clearly illustrated in his letter to Miss MacLeod in September 1895 when he wrote, "Let us work without the desire for name or fame or rule over others ... "

So it seems that being aware of one's own breath, sitting quietly in front of an icon, an artefact, a candle flame, a blank wall, using written words/letters as something divine, or simply letting the words of Holy Scripture dwell in the mind are all forms of meditation which still the mind, and are a great help in focusing our minds on what Einstein called "The great ocean beyond".

I have been blessed with sharing first-hand, many forms of meditation, with groups from different religions and also with psychologists and healers. Some with great faith, others with none.

For example, a year or more after my Sikh Gurdwara experience in 1991, I was allowing my mind to be washed in the calmness of the shrine room at the Ramakrishna Vedanta Centre, Bourne End, when my meditations became more empathetic, and I entered into a simple form of prayerful meditation.

I had just learned that the head of the Vedanta movement in the UK, Swami Bhavyananda, had died on the second of December, and I had been reflecting our walks together in his beautiful gardens, when one of the brothers, Joseph, entered the shrine. I felt strongly that I wanted to talk with him of the sad loss of his teacher whom he had served faithfully for the past decade.

I sat, and my spirit sent forth messages of warmth and understanding, sympathetic love to Joseph. I became more aware of the many symbolic parts of the ritual that he was performing:

The submission to the ideal of Ramakrishna.

The sprinkling of water.

The lighting of the candle.

The dipping into the oil.

The incensed induced flame and smoke.

The placing of the flower heads above the large icons of Ramakrishna, his wife and his disciple.

The rhythmic hand bell.

The great circles of the living glowing incense - as his arm performed devotional arcs before the icons.

Icons which cleansed the mind of idol worship, wealth creation, jealousness, aggression and all other forms of arrogant egocentricity, for all were but pointers to God ...

And I knew that I could well be experiencing the highest possible communication between human souls. Joseph who became Brother Atmachaitanya, now Swami Shivarupananda sent his soft, devotional, soundless words of loving acknowledgement across unknown waves of the spirit.

And I was filled with blessed awe at my understanding.

Meditation deals primarily with the realization of wisdom through the control and management of the mind. It is a system of physical, mental and spiritual development. It is a letting go, changing the perception of our world into a "soft focus" while making our Transcendental Awareness appear within our consciousness like an holographic "magic picture" forming out of the chaos of random patterns.

This then is the meditative approach to realizing Conscious Awareness and Transcendental Consciousness. Transcendental Consciousness only becomes manifest by the Grace of God. However, like so much of our lives that we take for granted, we are often ignorant of the Grace, but when it does enter into our meditations our consciousness itself becomes Grace-filled. And this is when we enter into true prayer.

PRAYER

IN THE LATE nineteen-eighties I went to a service in Llandaff Cathedral, and prayed that God would lead me to a better understanding of the Christian faith of my childhood. On the way out I came upon a leaflet that told of a Bible study with Victor Steele. Victor later told me that I must have found an old leaflet, as he had not put any out for a long time. Was this mere coincidence or was it an example of being part of the interconnected, synchronistic world we discussed in earlier chapters, where things naturally come together? Whatever it was, it changed my life, and eventually led me to blend my developing meditations with scripture, and with Christian prayers.

Although prayer can utilize meditation, it is, in some respects, a different, albeit related, paradigm. Effective prayer is an honest, sincere, humble, devoted attempt to communicate with the giver of our gift of life. It is a two-way communication that involves much objective listening and we must always be on our guard to avoid confusing the *act* of prayer, when we are simply addressing others, with the *state* of prayer, when we sincerely seek union with God.

True prayer is from the heart. Unfortunately, prayer can become divorced from the meditative grounding that is so necessary, turning communication with God into a form of poetry whose vibrations are only intended to reach our nearby neighbors.

Prayer then, is then an attempt to communicate directly with God.

Communication through prayer is usually in the form of language, which could be written, spoken or simply thought through. Prayer can, and does, extend beyond language to the ultimate indefinable harmonious, empathetic, all-knowing, understanding communication with the Ultimate Reality, God.

There are many recognized forms of prayer, from worshipful formal prayers, intercessionary prayers, to the spontaneous prayers of hope and despair.

An example of a devotional, explanatory and poetic prayer is to be found in the Mul Mantra of the Sikh scripture. It is taught to every Sikh child:

> "There is but one God. Truth is His Name, creative His personality and immortal His form. He is without fear, without enmity, unborn and self-illuminated. By the Guru's grace He is obtained."

(In this case Guru is synonymous with God)

There are those who listen for God in their prayers and sometimes record what has come to them. The founder of the Baha'i faith, Baha'u'llah, recorded in *The Hidden Words*,

> "With the hands of power I made thee and with the fingers of strength I created thee; and within thee I have placed the essence of My light … " Suggesting a divinity within each one of us that could be related to humanity being created in the "mage" of God.

There is the Christian prayer which often combines worship with requests, such as:

> "Our Father who is in Heaven, holy is your name. May your kingdom come, may your will be done, on earth as it is in Heaven. Give us this day our daily bread. Forgive us our wrong doings as we forgive those who do wrong against us, and lead us not into temptation but deliver us from evil".

There are spontaneous prayers, which many believe originate directly from a transcendental source, which for Christians is a communion with the Holy Spirit and includes such phenomena as, "the gift of tongues" as described by Saint Paul of the New Testament. Christians are told that when two or three are gathered together to pray, then God, in the form of Jesus Christ, will be present. These are often intercessionary prayers for personal and social needs. It is where healing has taken place.

However, for finding out our ultimate destiny it is the quiet, devotional, personal prayers, where deep truths can be uncovered, that are most important. It is the prayers between an individual and his or her creator. It is the prayer that Jesus advocates most of all. It is the prayer that links East and West. It makes no outward show to impress; it is wholly and completely between the Ultimate Reality, the Greater Consciousness, the Universal Divinity, the Real, the Personal Creator (or what ever else you choose to call God), and yourself. It is a submission in humble devotional openness without recourse to anyone else. It is private, personal and in human terms, secret.

How then, can we judge the effect of prayers? Does praying for a person make him or her live longer? As people who are prayed for often, such as the British royal family, do not live longer than "ordinary" people, it could be concluded that prayer is ineffective. But, surely any experiment designed to measure the result of prayer must be far more complex. We would need not only to measure the quantity of a person's life but also the quality, their inner calmness and their ultimate destiny. Even what may appear to be a simple task such as measuring quality is difficult, for it has components that are physical, mental and spiritual. It is not easy to decide just what it is that we should be measuring.

Dr. Michael Krucoffe, the Associate Professor of Medicine/Cardiology, and his team at Duke University Medical Centre in the USA has published many articles on the scientific evaluation of prayer, which shows some intriguing statistical significance of the value of prayer for physical and mental healing. However, his overriding results concerning the actual improvement of health for those who are prayed for, compared with those who are not, are inconclusive. Perhaps all scientific approaches are doomed to give indeterminate results, as our creator wishes prayer to have more significance than being used for "simple" scientific investigations?

Even so there are four obvious benefits of prayer.

Firstly, like the visualization techniques, relaxation tapes and meditation, prayer is therapeutic. Prayer has been widely reported to be medically beneficial to the person praying. The vibes produced by true prayer, within the mind of the 'pray-er', have a soothing, healing and strengthening effect.

Secondly, if you pray for others and they become aware of it, receptive recipients of your prayer will normally feel benefit. In praying for others you are thinking through their problems with love and compassion and understanding without being judgmental. This altruistic understanding can be healing in itself.

Thirdly, the spirit, mind and body are intimately linked. By praying, both the mind and consciousness of the person who is praying and that of the recipient become focused upon higher things. In some cases physical healing has been reported to occur.

Fourthly, one can become free of the idea that worldly aims and objectives are the only important goal in life and begin to see life in a fuller context. Benevolent or transcendental 'thoughts' can increase contentment and inner calm, while still taking part in our worldly activities.

All-in-all there is little doubt that prayer has, at the very least, a therapeutic human action on the mind of the person praying, and that true prayer can lift the mind towards the timeless transcendental truth. I do not pretend to know the upper boundary value of prayer, for it is unknowable. But I do believe that any one who receives sincere prayer will know much more about its value than the most learned observer.

Prayer is more than contemplation, for although contemplation can be a profoundly enriching experience, it need not have any transcendental component. To contemplate music, art or the setting sun is, I believe, nature's way for us to interact with our environment. It need have no outcome. It may herald prayer, but for most people the experience of contemplation is sufficient in itself and does not herald any truly profound transcendental experiences which illuminate our very *being* and the Creator of that *being*.

Prayer differs from meditation in that, in general, meditation is based upon improving our own spirituality, whereas effective prayer strives not only to feel compassion for others, but also seeks the opportunity to turn that compassion into fruitful action.

It was the end of October 1994, I had been invited to the East London Mosque in Whitechapel Road, and experienced a different view of the understanding of prayerful worship to God. God as revealed by Muhhammad. One of the main Mosque administrators, Chowdhury Mueenuddin, explained that Islam was encapsulated by, "Peace, through submission to Almighty God, whose name is Allah".

As Abdul Awwal, the Imam, led the prayers I was filled with great respect. I was witnessing a form of what could well have been absolute submission by individuals to God. A practice far removed from theory. Unfortunately, time did not allow me to discuss the historical problems that have arisen from religious charismatic leaders, who tap into sincere and intense devotion, only to lead people to seek the suffering and death of others. And what overruling selfless moral or spiritual reasons could there possibly be that allows half the population to remain in a subservient role?

It was during this time that I reflected on how my understanding had changed since I first visited the Reformed Cistercian Brothers at Caldey Island monastery, located off the coast of Tenby in South Wales. I was then in my early twenties. The experience changed my skepticism from believing that the monks were just a group of people cooperating for their particular brand of survival, to realizing that if mankind were relevant to some form of Creative Force, the most obvious form of communication would be by prayer. At the time I found myself inwardly thanking those monks for their prayers of intercession to God on behalf of us all.

I saw it as a sort of "belt and braces" approach, which might do me a bit of good if God were involved in my destiny. I reasoned that in the last analysis prayer could be the most worthwhile activity that people take part in. In those early years of manhood I thought that all prayer was formal, more of the mind and intellect rather than of the heart, reciting some prayer or other, often learnt by rote and not really understood. I see now that, although knowing a prayer is a tremendous asset, especially in times of difficulty, prayer itself has many more dimensions.

There are profound prayers that have come to some individuals, which gush forth like fresh springs into the knowledge pool of the human race; such as the amazing *Prayers Answered* which, I have been told, was written by an anonymous Confederate soldier of the American Civil War:

"I asked for strength, that I might achieve.
I was made weak, that I might learn humbly to obey.

I asked for health, that I might do greater things.
I was given infirmity, that I might do better things.

I asked for riches, that I might be happy.
I was given poverty, that I might be wise.

I asked for power, that I might have the praise of men.
I was given weakness, that I might feel the need of God.

I asked for all things that I might enjoy life,
I was given life that I might enjoy all things.

I got nothing that I asked for - but everything that I had
hoped for.

Almost, despite myself, my unspoken prayers were answered.
I am among all men, most richly blessed."

You may find that you too are blessed, or become blessed, with a gift of your own personal prayers.

At the Powys Prayer Conference in 1998, it came to me that prayer has many forms. There are those among us who pray in humility and receive in abundance. They are world class "pray-ers" who could be likened to Olympic athletes. There are the magnificent, restless, intercessory "prayer-warriors" who interface with the suffering world, and often put their own lives at risk in countries ruled by dictators or by a military junta. And there is the calmness of the peace-seeking monk.

It is to the peace-seeking monks and the prayer-warriors that we should be looking for guidance in our journey of prayer. I pray, that eventually the world will live in peace, in harmony, in love, in knowing, in sharing, and in worshipping that which created us, God. And if prayer has influence beyond the phenomenal part of our existence, then it could well be that many people praying together have an effect that is much greater than our individual prayer.

So what can we conclude about prayer? Just what is prayer in practice? Firstly, its true value cannot be sought through academic or philosophical means and it seems unlikely to be verified by science. As learning to swim requires us to enter into water, so we must immerse ourselves in the practice of prayer to begin to understand its value, first by listening to the prayers of others and then by practising prayer for ourselves, ideally surrounded by the worship of others.

My early prayer life started in earnest with a request for help, to alleviate some of my ignorance and suffering. It developed into requests for other's needs. But now it seems to be more like a never-ending stream of love and hope from my mind which seems to link the infinite and draw its life force from beyond and still be part of my very *being*. However, the bustle of daily life can still disrupt the flow.

Perhaps the thoughts that I had on April 25th 1996, and later dedicated to my little granddaughter Victoria, who died the following year, may shed a little more light on what prayer means to me now that I have been blessed to find a fuller faith in God:

> Ultimately prayer is the holding in your mind, at all times, compassion for another.
>
> It is like a small candle brightly shining in the background of your thoughts.
>
> It is empathetic and caring and naturally changes from a glow to a bright illumination of one's whole being when someone needs you to help or comfort him or her.
>
> And at all times God is your guiding companion.

In prayer it is not God who comes nearer to us but we who approach God. In combining meditation and prayer I have been able to obtain insights that are far beyond my own intellect and normal mental ability. It is a way of stepping out of the logical and innovative world of the mind and into a land of compassion, harmony, wisdom and love. In such a place we detect that faint sweet aroma of God's very breath.

MEDITATIVE PRAYER

MEDITATION AND PRAYER are different paradigms of the same spiritual continuum. Let me expand this idea a little more:

Meditation is excellent for finding that inner calm which is available within ourselves and thus is a good vehicle for understanding the reality of Self and *being*. For Carl Jung, the Self is the Universal Being that contrasts with the self of the personal or ego being. For me the Self is an expression for the divine spark that is within each of us, so that meditation becomes an attempt to reach, or realize, or be-at-one with, the ground of oneself, that is the divine spark that resides within each of us.

The peace that emanates from a truly spiritual person's meditation can help to bring peace and harmony to all. But for meditators this is often a secondary, or side effect. Its real aim is to purify the mind and bring peace to the person meditating.

Prayer is also excellent for inducing an inner calm, but it also invites the person praying to directly pray for peace in the world, along with the peace and well-being of others. However, unlike meditation, effective prayer is when we attempt to communicate directly with the divinity of the "all", the external, that which is all things, created all things and is beyond all things, that which I am referring to as God. Prayer invokes God, often asking for guidance and intervention.

Sikhs often express this relationship as practising *nam,* which is, "to practice the presence of the All Pervading Divine Spirit by keeping him ever in mind with love and devotion".

In the former, meditation, it is the Self which we aim to realize and become. In the latter, prayer, it is the way in which we go out to meet the Ultimate Divinity and then see this divinity in others. That is, the manifestation of prayers resonates with the divinity in which we are immersed. A more practical way of expressing the relationship that develops through prayer is to follow the profound example of the late Mother Teresa of Calcutta who saw the face of Jesus in all she met.

Whereas meditation by inference does not demand any action in the world on the part of the meditator, but rather a passive acceptance of the pain and pleasure of life, prayer attempts to remove all suffering by involving the grace of God, and by exercising the talents that have been gifted to us for action in the world. In general meditation is inward looking, while prayer outwards. But, as I hope I have conveyed in the last two sections of this chapter, there are many overlapping forms of prayer and meditation.

Prayer can be enacted by rote and through poetry where a good speaker can be more impressive than a tearful person of the spirit. Just how effective a prayer is, is not easy for us to determine, for it doesn't depend upon quality of voice or acting ability but as scripture suggests, "A good man's prayer is very powerful and effective" (James 5:6b). And a "good man" is a measure of the sincere altruistic compassion of the person praying from the heart; that is using the power of their inner divine spark.

Prayer and meditation in some respects start in opposite directions, but both are on the same transcendental plain. If you leave New York and travel due East for long enough you come to the same place as if you had initially traveled due West from New York. And so it is with meditation and prayer. But your experience during your journey has been different and so the outcome may be very different – from continued silence to energetic action for oneself or for others in the name of God.

As one yearns to directly communicate with God by seeking outwards in prayer we simultaneously and automatically move inwards towards our inner divine spark.

As one meditates by looking inwards, seeking to become conscious of, and merge with, the divine spark within, we simultaneously and automatically move outwards and become more and more aware of that from whence we came (God, the Tao, Brahman, the Greater Consciousness etc.).

Both meditation and prayer are like the two ends of a seesaw - if we try and move towards divine grace in one direction we automatically cause our awareness to move in the other, i.e. the more we become aware of God, the more we become aware of the divine within, and vice-versa.

Putting these ideas together I have found that the most profound prayer is meditative, purposely combining the inner *being* with the outer world and expecting God to be present, and to give a lead. It is a two-way communication with God that consists mainly of peaceful, expectant listening. Initially you will need to find that quiet room or space we have discussed previously, unplug the telephone, switch off the TV, move well away from the doorbell, and be all alone. The initial object is to still the mind, perhaps by slowly breathing in and out, and gently observing on one's own breath as in the Hatha yoga meditation.

With practice inner peace and prayerful meditation can be done in the noisiest of bustle that we experience in our modern world, and within one or two breaths deep stillness can come to the mind.

I sometimes find it useful to meditatively pray with my eyes open and looking straight ahead. This is something that I adapted from an original meditation taught to me by a Brahma Kumaris nun

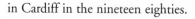

in Cardiff in the nineteen eighties.

Meditative prayer involves a true yearning of the heart, a seeking of God's advice. All inhibitions must melt away and we become filled with a longing humility simply to be guided by God. Words may form in the mind, but mainly we ask God for simple guidance, "Lord, show me your way". Then we rest in that null point of attentive peace. Sometimes there is nothing, at other times a profound insight occurs, beyond the normal powers of reasoning.

Prayer can be a request for guidance from God. I believe that God then chooses to act in the light of the prayer and in the totality of the universal purpose. Many ask why God allows this, or that, to happen. I have done so in the past myself, but then I ask myself whether it is it reasonable to always expect God to instantly jump to our requests, or demands, in the way that we believe would be of benefit to ourselves or others? After all, we respond to requests in many ways, often depending upon who asks, and the reason behind the request.

In some respects when we ask for God's assistance we are like children asking for sweets. A good parent will not always give a child what is asked for as they are aware of the long term needs of their protégé. Likewise God is often silent, but by our side. It seems that God, appears to be allowing us to discover for ourselves our ultimate destiny. For this purpose our lives are part of a complexity, a maze, with intertwining threads of pain and pleasure, suffering and joy.

With enduring yearning, love, and humility we find that our Conscious Awareness begins to grow, and truly awesome truths begin to seep in. In some respects the listening, in meditative prayer, reminds me of my research days when sometimes I would be relaxing and then quite unexpectedly a solution to a complex problem would make itself known in my conscious mind.

The inner consciousness must be awakened through the Grace of God. If God gives us a flash of divine light, all our doubts are destroyed. The nearer you approach God, the less you reason and argue. When you attain God then all sounds, all-reasoning and disputing, come to an end and you go into communion with God in silence.

Like a match struck in a room that has been in darkness for a thousand years, quite suddenly all will become clear.

Meditative prayer is when you form a thought in your mind and soundlessly address it to God, and wait humbly, timelessness being the essence. This timelessness is the pregnant silence before the inevitability of new birth.

Finding inner calm and peace should always precede prayer, and to find such peace is to find the divine spark within. This is best achieved by meditation. With practice this "centering on inner peace" can, as we have already mentioned, be achieved in the space of a few breaths. Then if we are so inclined we are ready to travel outwards to meet with God. This is meditative prayer, which is a communion of divinity both within and without and includes much silence.

There are many interpretations of meditative prayer, but I have come to see it as a progression. Firstly achieving inner calm, then to bodily resonance and healing, then to a re-affirmation of the reality of God, then to communion with God, and finally to action-based love.

I have found that many things have come to me in silence. One such gift is my own personal prayer, which came one line at a time over a period of two years. I quietly say this prayer to myself daily with periods of silence between each line:

"Dear God, thank you for bringing me here now ...
Thank you for all that I am and all that I have ...
Thank you for my gift of life, may I be worthy of the gift ...
Help me to be unattached, that I may act with love to all I
meet ...
Help me to persevere on the path of your purpose ... "

Perhaps this is the moment for me to ask you to stop a while and pray, and in your prayers pray for me and my work, for as I write this I am surely praying for you ...

There is of course much more we could explore in prayer and meditation, but it is time to move on to the next part of our journey.

If we believe that God is active in his world, we should use every legitimate means at our disposal to uncover the timeless truths embedded within our great world religious traditions. The primary source material for the wisdom of the ages today is, arguably, in the form of our inherited and revered sacred writings recorded in world scriptures, scriptures that have existed since the dawn of writing and are even now still being produced.

WORLD SCRIPTURES

WHAT IS SCRIPTURE? From *The Encyclopaedia of Religion*, "Scripture is the generic concept used in the modern West and, increasingly, worldwide, to designate texts that are revered as especially sacred and authoritative in all major and many other religious traditions".

The *Encyclopaedia* goes on to explain that scripture addresses the spiritual rather than the secular parts of our nature.

Religious texts are often supported by archaeological remains, works of art, and other evidence, but in every instance the real data of the religion resides in its texts.

How then can we rate a sacred text, such as the Zoroastrian Gathas? Are they simply historical sonnets, or do they contain within them an understanding of the reality of God? Does the writing reflect the word of God? Or actually contain the word of God?

One could argue that there are two major ways of approaching scriptural texts. The first is the academic approach, while the second is the way of meditative prayer. Even though they are independent, they are often complementary.

A typical academic stance was taken by William Mulandra who wrote, "Before one can begin to read a text intelligently, one must be able to place the text in a proper context, to discern its historical position, its authorship, its intention, and so on. The most frequent

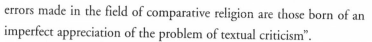

errors made in the field of comparative religion are those born of an imperfect appreciation of the problem of textual criticism".

It appears that with the academic approach we must consider factors such as dating, relative chronology, authorship, authenticity, human understanding, intelligence, emotion, political desire, social issues of the day, translations, writing errors, selection of canon, the language chosen, mode of composition and so on and so on. On top of all this, it is also clear that the history of some of the older religions is in an abysmal state of preservation.

Take, for example, the history of the Zoroastrian beliefs, as expressed in the Avesta (which through Judaism could have greatly influenced the writings and beliefs of Biblical and Qur-anic writers).

According to some analysts, Zarathustra (Zoroaster in Greek) lived out his life before the Iranians would have considered using writing as an acceptable way of recording sacred text. Early writing was considered as only suitable for the worldly things of art and commerce; it was feared that writing would degrade the spiritual reality of revealed truths as it did not demand that the reader adopted the "correct" attitude of mind before the information was given to him. The Avesta, which includes the Gathas, the Zoroastrian collection of holy texts, was finally set down in a specially invented alphabet in the fifth or sixth century BC. Except for the Gathas, all parts are anonymous. The composite works of generations of priestly poets and scholars, the Sasanian Avesta was a massive compilation in twenty-one books. Only a few copies were made, and in the destruction that followed the successive Greek, Arab, Turkish and Mongol conquests of Iran - all were destroyed. The surviving Avesta consists of liturgies, hymns and prayers. The original manuscript goes back to Sasanian times, but the oldest existing manuscript was only written down in the fourteenth century.

It seems that we can subdivide and analyze existing scripture forever more, but never know its historical authority. Did Zarathustra have true visions from God? Was he daydreaming, or a victim of his own delusions? Have the texts been so contaminated by mankind's ideals, goals, and ambitions that in the end they are meaningless in terms of understanding God? Expert opinion differs, so that we are not even sure if Zarathustra lived around 1,500 BC or a thousand years later!

There is no denying that genuine guidance aimed at helping our understanding and spiritual development can be of great value. However, by deciding for ourselves the meaning of any text and afterwards comparing it with the findings of others, we are less likely to be influenced (or some would say brainwashed), by extremists or fundamentalists. For it is my belief that many transcendental truths vibrate naturally with our very essence. And that essence, that divine spark, can only be accessed by seeking and receiving the Grace of God. As we read and wait we are, in fact, listening for God's words, and not our own.

Scriptural messages often have many levels of meaning. At times an academic can throw light on some seemingly ambiguous statement, helping to clarify our understanding of place, time, social context and words chosen by the translator. This could help us to realize the hidden message behind a clinically translated text. The academic approach can be helpful, providing we see that it limits us, by and large, to an understanding shaped by worldly considerations. All too often the academic does not include a transcendental dimension in their analysis; for transcendental experiences are intrinsically beyond words and difficult to quantify.

I have found that to shed a little more light on the value of our world scriptural texts I have had to turn away from the academic to a second method, the way of meditative prayer. This second method can still utilize all the academic knowledge that we have accumulated, but first we have to free our minds of worldly things, advice made quite clear in the Gospel of Ramakrishna,

"What will it avail a man to have mere scholarship? A pundit may have studied many scriptures, he may recite many sacred texts, but if he is still attached to the world and inwardly he loves 'women and gold', then he has not assimilated the contents of the scriptures. For such a man the study of scriptures is futile." A suitable non-academic approach is to use a form of meditative prayer that seeks to involve God's love.

First we have to decide whether to attempt to read the texts in their original language (Sanskrit, Hebrew, Greek, Arabic etc) or use a particular translation. I chose to seek out English-based translations simply because it would take me too long to learn all the relevant languages and gain an in-depth understanding of all the related cultures. Before choosing a particular rendering or translation of any of the great scriptures, I took considerable care and sought much advice from those who practice the faith, rather than taking the course suggested by academics. I was very aware of the problems of translations due to history and the pervading cultures down the ages. I was not seeking the literal, but the prophetic and spiritual message of the sacred texts.

Typical of this process is the way in which I became the owner of eight volumes of the Sikh scripture, the *Sri Guru Granth Sahib ji*, translated by Manmohan Singh.

I was at a Christian-Sikh conference in London in 1992, when four prominent Sikhs discussed my needs at some length. Then, spearheaded by Dr Harcharan Singh Sahni, they proceeded to find the first four volumes of the scripture that very day; the remaining four volumes came direct from the sacred city of the Sikhs, Amritsar, in the Punjab.

I have used this personal approach for finding suitable translations and versions of sacred texts such as *the Bible*, the *Qur-an*, the *Upanishads*, the *Dhammapada*, the *Bodhisattva* and the *Bhagavad-Gita*. All have their story.

To obtain the true flavor of world scriptures we must desire to be in the presence of the transcendental. Can established religion aid us in our task? Yes, it can, but again we have to be on our guard for each group Hindu, Sikh, Christian, Muslim, Jew, and so on, all have diversity within them; for it is apparent that *all* religions have, to a greater or lesser extent, succumbed to human influence, resulting in a variation of "truth". It is a very sobering thought that without such influence there would be only one set of beliefs within each religious order, and perhaps one belief system, but this is definitely not so.

A very powerful form of meditative prayer is what many call Lectio Divina, and like all powerful tools it must be used with care and respect. Asking for God's guidance is necessary before we even start, so that we can separate out God's word from our own. When reading, praying and meditating on scripture we should be asking ourselves: As all creation is, in the widest sense, a measure of God's selfless giving, is the scripture, that we are reading, advocating selfless giving? Does it contain inspiration that reveres God? Are they the *actual* words of God, or are they the words of man, his politics, his ambitions and his ego? Are the words asking me to fulfill human aims; are they simply the mission statements of some historical or contemporary human leader? Are our own interpretations of scripture being contaminated through the imperfections of our own mind?

Well, it turned out that I had been using the meditative prayer, *Lectio Divina*, for many years without realizing it. It had in fact been a method practiced by many before me to uncover God's deeper messages. I first heard of *Lectio Divina* from the reverend Melvyn Matthews at Ammerdown (a retreat centre just outside Bath, UK) who told me that Father William Shannon in his book *Seeking the Face of God*, presents us with a way of praying which is inspired by the work of Thomas Merton. He develops the idea of the spiritual ladder from the work of the Carthusian monk Guigo II, who died in 1188. Guigo tells us that there are four rungs on the ladder by which we are lifted up to heaven.

Lectio Divina, I suspect, is the normal way that a devout person has always read, meditated and prayed on higher thoughts, even if the term itself was not known. It counteracts our hunger for worldly possessions and the more modern worship of *information* itself, (when intoxicating images and worldly facts can easily swamp us).

In *Lectio Divina* we must attempt to stop and absorb, to bring into the text its original art, music and poetry, but most of all, its spiritual message.

To understand great things we must savor them. Like a good wine, we do not simply gulp it down and call for more. We take in its aroma, roll it around the tongue, imagine its history and relate it to the good things in life. *Lectio Divina* is a method of savoring scripture. Popularized by Saint Benedict in the early Middle Ages, it is a simple approach, consisting of four movements (Guigo's four rungs on the ladder by which we are lifted up to heaven), taking us from reading the word of scripture, through meditation on its meaning for us, to spontaneous prayer, and then to a silent presence of God in love.

To begin, quiet the mind and body, bringing scattered energies into focus. The first phase of *Lectio Divina* is *Lectio*, a prayerful reading, or listening to, the words of God. Choose a passage, story, or parable from scripture. Read slowly and receptively engage your mind with the word. Let the words saturate and move through like slow, gentle rain. Let words or phrases repeat themselves. I often like to read a page or so, and come back to a sentence, or even a word that *resonates* within me.

For example, consider the Biblical text, "Jesus answered, 'The first is, Hear, O Israel: the Lord our God, the Lord is one; you shall love the Lord your God with all your heart, and with all your soul, and with all your mind, and with all your strength. The second is this, you shall love your neighbor as yourself'."

When a word or passage touches you, gradually let yourself be drawn into *Meditatio*, a reflection on the reading. Ponder the word, or phrase, or sentence, and become aware of its meaning for you. Think about its personal message, noticing how it speaks to the here and now, how it calls out for some attitude or action. Struggle with any conflicts it creates within, until calmness descends once more.

As you are meditating you may become consciously aware of a response. This is the third movement or *Oratio*, where your heart is touched in prayer. You may experience a deep longing, gratitude, repentance, intercession, wonder, regret or oneness; all moments of Grace-filled consciousness. Each of us will be as the Spirit moves us.

The Biblical scripture above, concerning "loving God and one's neighbor" gave me the understanding that, to love my neighbor, I must first love myself; but to truly love my own characteristics, I find that I need to be a better person. For me, this implies being in close communion with God, and I have found myself praying to become a person more worthy of the gift of this life that I have been granted. At another time - when I have been feeling particularly vulnerable and self-critical, I have realized that I need to be kind to myself before I can be kind to others. Leading to the awesome oneness as I just *be*.

The last stage of *Lectio Divina* is *Contemplatio*, a silent resting in God's presence - allowing all language and thoughts to dissolve and dwell wordlessly in the heart. To experience and accept being loved by God.

Separating the phases of *Lectio Divina* makes it is easier for us to understand, but in practice it should be a seamless progression that may be different each time. We follow what we are moved to follow. The sacred reading tunes us, or opens us, to a gift of deeper understanding. We cannot know beforehand what the result will be.

In using *Lectio Divina* we are no longer analyzing the scripture, but allowing a filtering and purification of our thoughts to occur naturally.

This process was, I believe, fully understood by the ancient Celts as *The Book of Kells*, suggests. I can thoroughly recommend a visit to see for yourself this inspired and pictorially elaborate book kept at Trinity College, Dublin. It is an original calligraphy of the four gospels of the New Testament.

With these thoughts in mind, it is perhaps a little easier to sympathize with the reluctance of the priestly tribe of ancient Iran, the Magi, to use writing as a means of communicating sacred words. For writing could be read by anyone without any deeper understanding. Initially the writing of scripture used a form of cipher, or code, that would only be known to a select few.

Literal interpretations of scripture often detract from its original message. For by definition, scripture is about the transcendental, or spiritual, world; a world we cannot touch, or see and has to be described by analogy and metaphor to convey an underlying meaning. For example, in the Jewish Pentateuch we are told that when resolving a grievance we should be thinking along the lines of, "An eye for an eye, a tooth for a tooth, a hand for a hand, a foot for a foot. A burn for a burn, an open wound for an open wound, a bruise for a bruise" (*Exodus* 21:24-26).

In some parts of the world the above text will still be interpreted as being the literal truth from God and must be obeyed to the letter. Others, such as an Orthodox rabbi, using the Talmud, may well come to a conclusion that the compensation for the victim should be the *value* of an eye. But is such justice from God or man? Where are love, compassion and forgiveness?

CONSOLIDATION

SINCE I WAS a teenager I have enjoyed my visits to the great pebble beach at Cold Knap, in South Wales. A few years back I found myself visualizing that vast crescent pebble beach as the fullness of our understanding of God. Some only pick up one of the pebbles and analyze it in meticulous detail – and start believing that the particular pebble they are examining is superior to all the others. However, it is not the pebble that is important but the beach itself. We cannot confine God to our particular form of understanding and deny God's existence in other pebbles. For each pebble on its own tells us little of the shape of the beach. The whole bach exceeds the sum of its parts. The beach is of pebbles but a pebble does not shape the beach. It is the beach that shapes the pebble.

When reading scripture it is tempting to seek to verify the existence of God from fulfilled predictions, miraculous happenings, and concepts of our origins that can be verified by today's science. These things may be fascinating but searching for this sort of "proof" can distract us from finding the underlying message, whereas I believe that true scripture tells us to give selfless love to all we meet, even if we disagree with their actions and morals. True scripture illustrates God's love in his creation; it emphasizes the importance of *being*, it points us to worship.

And although each revered scripture reflects the convention and understanding of the society of its time, there is a great similarity in their underlying messages. *It is this common base that underlines their authenticity.* Take the following examples:

The Gospel of Zarathustra concentrates the mind on One God and the importance of improving the world by daily action.

The Bhagavad-Gita is an incredible story of the dichotomies of the practical world, through which we can glimpse some transcendental truths.

The Holy Bible is filled with the harshness of history along with prediction, prophesy, poetry, ethics, law and the love of God.

The Gospel of Sri Ramakrishna is very much an experiential document, which centers on the possibility of the realization of God while in this life.

The Holy Qur-an is in prescriptive form, tackling God's desires for our daily life.

Sri Guru Granth Sahib ji is a beautiful love poem to God.

The Dhammapada points us towards the ultimate journey within. (Gautama Buddha spoke little of the reality of God, as he was more interested in helping us all to follow a spiritual path).

The Vedantic Upanishads are profound and all embracing, especially in attempting to define the greater and lesser "characteristics" of God.

Each has its own way of imparting the message of the transcendental truth. We learn from *The Gospel of Ramakrishna*, "In the scriptures you will find the way to realize God. But after getting all the information about the path, you must begin to work. Only then can you attain your goal". The Sikh's scripture, the *Sri Guru Granth Sahib ji*, tells us that scriptures are but the tip of the iceberg and there is much more to learn.

The scriptures are like maps, which show you where to go to reach your goal. Just as there is much more to motoring than having a map, so there is much more to understanding the transcendental, the grace of God, than relying absolutely on the scriptures. Ultimately the journey to our destiny has to be undertaken alone. Too many people, especially Western theologians, spend all their time discussing the map; in fact we must all be careful not to spend excess time revering the map at the expense of the journey.

When the way is clear and well known, it could be that maps are no longer required. But again we have to proceed with caution, for there are many side roads and unknown paths that confront us as we journey through life and a good map, like good scripture, has all these features found within it.

Over the centuries there have been many ways that great people of God have come closer to God's truth using methods of contemplation, meditation and prayer. One was Saint Ignatius Loyola (1491-1556) who, after great suffering and depression finally surrendered, to love and to serve, God through Christ. He completely changed his life as a great Spanish soldier to become the founder of the Jesuit movement. His approach had much in common with *Lectio Divina* and the way of Saint Francis of Assisi.

To discern God's will, Saint Ignatius tells us that we must first go to a place where we feel the presence of God, realize that in this fallen world God welcomes all repenting sinners, travel with Christ to see where God is leading, feel the passion of Christ's suffering and ask ourselves even with such suffering in the world, if we are still going to respond in love. He found God in all things.

Before we journey further, this may well be a good time to pause and experience meditative prayer for yourself. Find any available book of scripture and take it to a quiet place, make your self comfortable, pause, take a few deep breaths and become at one with God, then open up the book, and with the love of God within you quietly absorb a short passage, close your eyes and let the words dwell within you, and wait in silence; ask only that God's love and compassion leads you to the truth.

It is initially good to practice *Lectio Divina* for ten minutes everyday for several consecutive days, rather than starting with long periods. The ideal time is first thing in the morning; try getting up ten minutes early and afterwards carrying on with your normal day. As the days pass you will find more and more meaning developing within your life. I can only urge you to try to start right now and again first thing tomorrow morning – this book will still be available when you return ...

I have found meditative prayer a wonderful way of beginning to understand God's presence in all human activity, especially when I use *Lectio Divina* in conjunction with reading world scriptures. The following sixteen extracts are a small representative sample of the many that have shone out to me in my daily readings of scripture over the last fifteen years or so.

There are those which concern our daily life:

1. "Perform your duties in the world but keep your mind always fixed on God". [*The Gospel of Ramakrishna.*]

2. " ... to make him who is an enemy a friend, to make righteous him who is wicked, and to make the ignorant learned". [*The Gospel of Zarathustra.*]

3. " ... Fearlessness; purification of one's existence; cultivation of spiritual knowledge; charity; self-control; performance of sacrifice; study the (scriptures) ... austerity; simplicity; non-violence; truthfulness; freedom from anger; renunciation; tranquility; aversion to faultfinding; compassion for all living entities; freedom from covetousness; gentleness;

modesty; steady determination; vigor; forgiveness; fortitude; cleanliness; and freedom from envy and from the passion for honour - these transcendental qualities ... belong to godly men endowed with divine nature." [*The Bhagavad-Gita.*]

4. "Like the lamp, you must shed light among your fellows, so that, when they see the good you do, they may give praise to your Father in heaven." [*The Holy Bible.*]

5. "But the Messenger, and those who believe with him, strive and fight with their wealth and their persons ..." [*The Holy Qur-an.*]

6. " ... Praise thou the Lord God's Name and also the true deeds ..." [*Sri Guru Granth Sahib ji.*]

7. "Meditate. Live purely. Be quiet. Do your work, with mastery ..." [*The Dhammapada.*]

8. "The wise man should merge his speech in his mind, and his mind in his intellect. He should merge his intellect in the Cosmic Mind, and the Cosmic Mind in the Tranquil Self." [*The Vedantic Upanishads.*]

And then there are scriptural passages that recognize the awesomeness of God:

1. "God alone is real. Make an effort to cultivate love for Him and find out the means to realize Him." [*The Gospel of Ramakrishna.*]

2. "Thou art the Holy Father of this Spirit who created all this joy-giving earth ..." [*The Gospel of Zarathustra.*]

3. "You are the supreme primal object. You are the ultimate resting-place of this entire universe. You are inexhaustible, and You are the oldest. You are the maintainer of the eternal religion, the Personality of the Godhead ..." [*The Bhagavad-Gita.*]

4. "Ascribe to the Lord. O heavenly beings. Ascribe to the

Lord glory and strength. Ascribe to the Lord the glory of his name; Worship the Lord in holy splendor." [*The Holy Bible.*]

5. " ...The Truth is from your Lord ..." [*The Holy Qur-an.*]

6. " ... The Lord's glory is pervading in ten directions and His worth I can utter not ... I am a sacrifice unto (God) ... who has laid the eternal foundation ... " [*Sri Guru Granth Sahib ji.*]

7. " ... He moves with love among the unloving ... Possessing nothing ... Wanting nothing." [*The Dhammapada.*]

8. " ... (Those) regarding sacrifices and humanitarian works as the highest, do not know any higher good." [*The Vedantic Upanishads.*]

The examples in each of the above groups are from different world scriptures, and if we possessed only these fragments it would be quite difficult to ascertain their origin, but not their truth.

And so we come to the point where we leave behind our last base camp and prepare for the final ascent. Now we take only essential equipment; truth seeking reason, an understanding of oneness and our *being*, carrying the burden and the suffering of others, but being aware of the closeness of God through the practice of meditative prayer.

CHAPTER 6

THE LAND OF ETERNITY

FROM CREATION TO DESTRUCTION

THE HINDU SYMBOL that represents the three aspects of God as the Universal Creator (Brahma), the Preserver (Vishnu), and the Destroyer (Shiva) is one simple letter similar to the number 3.

This ancient way of considering God is very appealing for an engineering scientist such as myself, for it clearly embodies the concept of time past, time present and time future, which illustrates the limits of scientific proof, inasmuch as it clearly separates out the only time in which we can verify the laws of our physical universe. This is because it is only in 'time present' that first order scientific proof can take place, 'time past' and 'time future' will only yield pointers to truth for direct experiments cannot be carried out in past or future time frames, as we discussed in earlier chapters. Incidentally such ancient philosophical understanding as found in the Hindu symbol, also illustrates the value of meditative prayer where timeless truths have been revealed through religious seers and prophets humbly seeking the divine.

The founder of the Sikh religion, Guru Nanak, on realizing that it was partial knowledge that had led to a multiplicity of practices, enhanced this Hindu symbol by adding a figure 1 in front of it, and a curve around this ancient sign for God, thus emphasizing that, no matter how complex, there was only one God who was united and limitless.

The beliefs concerning these three main aspects of God can be summarized as:

God the Universal Creator initiates everything within the time/space cosmos. Without God's influence there is nothing; from nothing the universe is created. God is above and apart from, yet within all creation, and every living thing breathes the breath of God.

God the Preserver keeps everything going. This aspect of God ensures that the laws of nature and science are maintained. Here God is seen as the wellspring of our scientific and technological discoveries. He ensures that things repeat in the same manner as before; thus all the natural laws that seem to "just exist", are in fact ensured by God's role as the Preserver.

God the Destroyer is seen as the god of death, allowing life to evolve anew. God recycles everything ready for more creation. In the whole universe only one *physical* thing can exist in one space at one time, hence the destructive action of God is more a form of "cleaning up" to claim space for the next happening. Seen in human terms; the Somme battlefields during the First World War were at one point in time oozing with mud, blood, slime and tens of thousands of rotting corpses. Today those very same fields, just one "God-moment" later, are green, lush and bursting with new life.

This simple, but all-embracing, model of Creation, Preserver, and Destroyer (CPD) illustrates how little we truly understand God's purpose - especially such horrors as the Somme battlefields. In facing such vivid truths I hope that we can progress our ideas beyond such terrible suffering to glimpse life's true purpose.

The CPD model illustrates quite clearly where science is at its most productive, that is in the here and now associated with the Preserver aspect of God. For it is in this mode, and this mode only, that science is able to carry out definitive, first order experiments. Whereas with things that have been created in the past (Creator aspect of God) or in the realms of the future (Destroyer aspect of God) science has little or no advantage over religious models, so that ultimate truth in these two areas could well be found through religious revelation rather than scientific innovation.

The four following sections briefly visit aspects of the CPD model. Although we have discussed in some detail the first aspect, Creation, there are a few more pointers to consider. These will be found in the next section, "The Creative Spirit". For the Preserver, the here and now so to speak, we will take two bites of the cherry, the first will be found in the section, "The Down Side"; while the second is discussed in the section, "Waves". The Destructive action of God I have called "The End Game".

THE CREATIVE SPIRIT

THIS RELATES TO the first, or Creative, aspect of God. But first I would like to add one or two personal thoughts before we journey on.

The whole of human existence will be here for only a moment of universal time, like a match struck in brooding blackness, life has flared up, it now burns brightly, but it will inevitably leave eternity once more to the featureless darkness of a cosmological night. But, the miracle is that life has "flared up", which leads some of us to ask, *Why?*

Could the ecologically based, ethical aims encompassed by an old Native American proverb be giving us vital clue? "We do not inherit the Earth from our ancestors. We borrow it from our children." This proverb suggests to me that best we can do in this world is to work to ensure that future generations find true wisdom and experience great joys.

Could it be as the Zoroastrians, Hindus, Jews, Christians, Muslims, Sikhs and others believe that it needs the Grace of God to come to us before we finally attain an understanding of our true destiny? If the latter is true, and I believe that it is, then it seems logical to strive to be as near as possible to God. To come close to God, we are told time and time again by scriptures that this means knowing oneself more fully. Saint Augustine of Hippo understood this all too well when he said:

"I have wandered away from myself.

I could not find myself

And much less could I find you (God)."

The most miraculous part of Creation is our own unique self, our personal non-exchangeable *being*. A thought that came to me in the pregnant silence of an early morning prayer, encapsulates this miracle:

"In the soft warm comfort of my mother's womb my individuality was born. In the quietness of eternity I *became* ...

Later my tranquillity was disturbed by gentle movements and muffled sounds that came from beyond my utter luxury. Could there be *other*? I stretched out my limbs. I strained my senses. But nothing, only the comforting *now*.

Then came the great upheaval. Thrust into a tunnel of gloom. Shocked into blinding light. Slapped into tears. Warmness of bodily love and soft, milk-filled breasts. Soon I became caught in the web of life. I felt. I moved. I grew. I learned. I abused. I gathered. I yearned. Again ... and again ... and again ...

A blessed pause; now complete cooperation in the entwining, bodily-love of another.

Then once more into the spirals of knowledge and more unknowing; all was shrouded in the mists of life's womb. My mind a captive, held spellbound. All seemed to be within a viscous binding fluid of never ending fun, fear, beauty, pain, excitement and information.

Faint sounds and thoughts gradually became clearer until I realized that, "From Super Strings to galaxies; flesh to spirit; life to death; grief to ecstasy - all is One. All is you, Lord - for at times I see you peeping around the veil of my existence and smiling".

And I cry out, "Don't you see? Can't you feel? Don't you understand?" But so much of the world seems to pass on by without a second glance.

THE DOWN SIDE

WHAT POINTERS TO the meaning of our lives can we find in the action of God as a Preserver?

How can we answer the suffering world where a child dies every three seconds in Africa; a world where seventy percent of the male adults in some primitive tribes are killed in conflict; a world where as I write this, two hundred countries are engaged in some form of war?

Where, in all this, do we find morality, justice and care?

Could all the suffering and death be caused by a demonic world, under the influence of an intelligent evil agent which many call the Devil? There certainly seems to be some worldly truth in the way Dante pictured Hell.

In India, devils have a habitation and a name.

Jainism provides an example of the many topologies of devils. The seven netherworlds contain the hells, one of which, the Vyantarus, includes demons, goblins, ghosts and spirits.

Anthropological studies show that Buddhism, particularly in Burma and Thailand, supports the concept of devilish beings, some of which cause pain. Buddhism has a devil called Mara.

Hindu lore has demonic beings that roam about at night, disturb, harass and kill people and some that frequent cremation grounds. However, Hinduism does not seem to acknowledge a specific leader of evil or a devil figure.

By contrast, in Islam the demons teach humans magic, lead people to unbelief, try to eavesdrop on heaven, and cause "unbelievers" to remain obstinate.

To Zoroastrians the devil rallies around his standard which, is the "evil thought" in people's minds.

Exorcism designed to "free" people from evil possessions has been associated with Christian evangelizing since its inception. And the Bible certainly points to an external manifestation, "For this enemy of yours, the devil, goes around like a lion, roaring in fierce hunger, seeking whom he may devour" (*1 Peter* 5:8).

A clear view of the possibility of an evil force was presented to me in May 1997 when I was walking the slopes of the bluebell-carpeted wooded "Valley of the dilapidated Thirteen Cottages", in the Brecon Beacons National Park in Wales. I was with a good friend of mine, Mike Ranstead, formally a charismatic evangelical leader of a House Church in Swindon, England which he and his wife Anne had started some thirty years or so previously.

After considerable encouragement from myself, he told me that he had witnessed, and later found he could apparently talk to, evil spirits within people. And when, in the right circumstances, they were told to, "Come out in the name of Jesus", the persons in whom the evil force had dwelt, could become gripped by uncontrollable physical spasms. Some people were thrown bodily across the room, before becoming free of their suffering.

In my late teens I spoke to a very happy and balanced farm housewife who was convinced that she had many times in the past confronted a poltergeist in a passage of an old farm. She explained in detail how such things as a jug full of water would be lifted off a tray and smashed to pieces.

The much-revered, nineteenth- century Guru, Ramakrishna, saw a black evil spirit leaving his body.

I have myself experienced circumstances where honest and open country people were induced to believe lies. Lies were caught like a disease spreading through the village, affecting the minds of normally welcoming and peace-loving people. A Christian friend later told me that lies are one of the first signs of evil manifesting itself.

There certainly seems to be evil at work when the politically motivated (often under the guise of religion), work behind the scenes to "inspire" the young, the vulnerable and the sincere to willingly in a bid to kill others die.

All this evil could, in fact, just be the natural background to existence. A volcano, a tornado or a flood does not have malice, it is not an intelligent entity, it kills indiscriminately.

And what do we make of a "loving" God who allows a child to be born in poverty, suffering from AIDS, in the middle of an African war? A child who spends a few miserable years and then dies in agony? Perhaps she experienced a little of the beauty of the world? Perhaps she caused love and tears to flow in others? The apparent unwarranted suffering of others certainly cause compassion to well up in me!

But in all truth, we seem to be back on the unlevel playing field of life. We are born unequal, and live unequal lives. But what if we start seeing our lives as a gift, *taking the existence of a lifeless grain of sand as our base line.* Life is not to be measured against perfection. For who are we to demand of our creator a perfect gift? If it were my birthday, not even my best friend would appreciate me complaining about the inadequacy of her gift. A gift of life is a gift, and we must start from that fact, rather than comparing ourselves with some ideal of perfection. There can be no perfection in a physical, time-dependent universe like ours.

It could be that another good friend of mine, Keith Lewis, is on the right track when he told me as we strolled by the salmon filled waters of the river Usk in the Welsh hills of Brecon, "An all-powerful

God has a plan which allows Satan, the Devil, his day". Why not a devil, a human-sized - not a God-sized - devil? In Keith's scenario, the devil would be merely another aspect of the human condition that God has provided for mankind to do battle with, to overcome, and in so doing have the possibility of evolving and becoming more as God would wish. In this case, I could well imagine the devil being an analogy for our internal struggle to overcome our hate, greed, anger, selfishness and covetousness.

The illness, poverty and great need in the world could be said to, "encourage our altruistic tendencies to blossom". Even out of the conflict of war has come great goodness, for much of our modern technological advancements started in a military environment.

Could it be that God allows such terrible things so that we learn to awaken our compassionate spirit; to care for our neighbor, no matter what his politics, nationality, race, religion or even his private morals?

One of the major underlying global problems to be solved is that of inequality. Was the looting that occurred during the early "liberation" of Basra and Baghdad in Iraq in 2003 a form of anarchy, or was it the underprivileged taking a slice of the fat man's cake? World disasters might prove to be the trigger that wakes up humanity, into a brotherhood of care and compassion. For as we evolve, cooperation, understanding, commitment and a much fairer sharing of the world's wealth will need to come about if we are to become a truly integrated human race where every individual combines authority with responsibility and freedom with joy.

Much of humanity is on the move, from family groups to tribes, to small kingdoms, to nations and even to the eventual possibility of global integration when such as the United Nations encompasses all peoples in some form of democracy. Could humanity be metamorphosing into a new and higher level of complexity? Cooperation has produced the great herds on the African plains.

Communication and cooperation must have been occurring with neighboring, single-cell life forms until a synchronistic event took place and a new level of complexity emerged in the form of multi-cellular life.

Evolution has always groaned under conflict until enlightened cooperation takes place, then a synergy occurs, and evolution jumps to the next stage of complexity. Evil is like a catalyst that causes a sharpening, as steel sharpens steel. We need to step back to see a bigger picture that is beyond our daily lives, a vision that is calling out to us to develop a compassion far more profound than the everyday love and help we naturally offer to our family, friends and comrades. To show love and compassion beyond self-preservation of ourselves, our genes or our species could well be the subliminal message of evil.

Was it conflict that encouraged cells and animals to respond to each other's needs, to cooperate and so evolve to a higher level of complexity? We have certainly witnessed much conflict in human societies as we become larger and larger groups living together.

Then again as we are now we are well on the way to developing worldwide communication, perhaps global cooperation is becoming an evolutionary possibility? All we need now is authentic freedom of speech, true altruistic compassion, mutual cooperation and care for each individual's needs!

THE END GAME

ON THE 27TH July 1992 Jeanette and I were visiting an old friend, Bob, just after his beautiful, wife, Esme, had unexpectedly died of cancer, at the age of forty-nine. In his anguish he blurted out many things. At one point I recollect him saying, "What happens if I marry again, who will I be with in the, so called, next life? - I want to be with Esme". Jeanette told how Jesus had explained such things about a woman who had married seven times and each time her husband had died. He said, "In the resurrection men and women do not marry, they are like angels in heaven" (*Matthew* 22:30). I leant on my scientific knowledge, intimating the possibility that time itself could be so segmented that many seeming impossibilities could be contained in simultaneous parallel time frames.

Meanwhile, eight-year-old Neena, a little Sikh girl who was staying with us at the time, was quietly tugging on my left sleeve. I reluctantly turned to her, and smiled - expecting a request for the toilet, but no, a clear crystal of truth came from the child's lips, "For God all things are possible". Her simple statement was the most profound, and the most helpful. And I was reminded that it is from the mouths of children that we often learn a deeper truth.

Sooner than most of us wish, we will have to face our own death. The very first death that I witnessed was that of my father. Just *before* he died I could feel his hesitant spirit gathering together to such an extent that I said quietly to my sorrowing mother, "He's going now, Mum". Moments later, as he exhaled his last breath, I sensed his very essence leaving his body in a great surge of energy, departing through the top of his head and shooting tangentially out into space. What was it that I witnessed in those last moments? I knew nothing of death, and I had certainly never heard anyone describe death like that!

We do not need to ask, 'Will we die?' We know we will. We rarely ask when and how we will die. Do any of us know if it will be in the next five minutes, or in many decades time? It is a sobering thought that well over ten people would have died somewhere in the world while you are reading the first half of this sentence. On average, twelve thousand will die of starvation alone in the next *hour*.

With medical science advancing so rapidly we can easily be lulled into a false sense of security concerning our own death. Death is not something that only happens to others. Sooner or later, it will profoundly affect each and every one of us.

Even the death of an unknown animal can cause us to feel pain. I remember when I was with my son, Jonathan, walking the bleak Norfolk coast in winter. We came across a dying sea bird, a gannet I believe. We felt sympathy for it, and wanted to comfort it, and save its life. But the bird was very weak, and help was far away. We sat for a while warming it with our body heat. The bird appeared to be contented, its whole body rhythmically rising and falling with each sighing breath. We left it hovering in that colorless world between harmonious life and disjointed death. It seemed to be peacefully accepting, waiting.

With hope we returned a short while later, only to find that it was dead.

Why should good people die before their expected time? I remember my cousin, Eric, dying from a heart attack at the modest age of fifty-seven. He was a caring man, with a loving wife and two dependent children, running a thriving small firm of twenty employees.

Why should my delightful nine-year-old granddaughter, Victoria, die? Why did her mother, her brother and her wider family have to suffer such a loss?

My experience tells me that the Creator of *me* personally has given me a chance to exist, and my life is a gift. But why the gift for some lasts longer than for others I do not know. Yet the gift of life, any life, is still more, much more, than existing as a lifeless grain of sand!

Life, in some respects, is like the beautifully intricate and temporary sand art of Buddhist monks. They work so hard for hours and sometimes many days, to create great beauty, using fine grains of colored sand. When it is complete they simply pour it onto the dusty earth. They tell us that our rewards come during our *actions*, not from the permanency of results. So, as I prepare for my last, and inevitable, journey into the dusty earth, the message seems to be that I should always try to fully experience and enjoy life, while still being aware of its impermanence.

It was September 2001 when I saw a cousin of mine. His wife of forty-four years, had died the afternoon before. With tears welling up in his eyes, he asked me why she suffered so much. Her cancer first showed up as a rash, then as a form of breast cancer, finally spreading throughout her whole body. In the last months she had fallen and broken her leg and arm. After hospitalization she had had the added misfortune to fracture her other leg while at home. She was in great agony in the last few weeks before she died. Such an active, giving, uncomplaining woman found it hard to ask others for help.

The Christmas before she died she insisted that all her grown up family of four, their partners and children, went to her home for Christmas. She did not tell them of her illness. Some were mystified, some were reluctant, but they all went. Then a few weeks before she died the family learned the truth. From then to the end of her life there was always someone by her side caring for her day and night, willingly, with unbounded love and compassion. There was nothing that they would not do to help her, comfort her and visibly demonstrate their love for her.

When an illness or accident is life-threatening, or when a friend or relative dies, it brings into sharp focus the value of our own life. It may help us to concentrate our mind so that we face up to our own death, and hence influence the way we live our lives, which in turn could affect our ultimate destiny. For surprisingly it is our grief, sadness, loneliness, fear and all forms of suffering that can, and often does, trigger thoughts beyond our earthly life. When a problem arises with a loved one, we remain alert, we care and comfort, we weep, we move to a higher plane of thought. And this can develop our compassionate altruistic love to embrace all.

And what happens to us once we are dead? Nothing? Heaven? Hell? Nirvana? Re-birth? I confess that I do not know. Perhaps my belief, at present, is best illustrated by the answer I gave to my ninety-four-year-old mother who asked me not long before she died, 'What *will* happen to me when I die?' Her question surprised me and I found myself embroidering on stories she had told me of her visits to Hereford market as a child. It went something like this:

> "When you were a little girl, Mum, you have told me that you went with your mother to Hereford market to sell her home-churned and shaped butter pats which were wrapped in dock leaves ... can you remember when you first went? It all seemed rather a scary place, with its bustle and noise and people towering above you? You did not know where you were or where you were going; it was all a great mystery.
>
> But, if you held onto your mother's hand you knew that everything would be all right.
>
> Well, Mum, when you die, just hold onto the hand of God and you will be all right."

We should live our lives in joy, but also in the knowledge of our inevitable death, for some *unknown* day we will not have a tomorrow. We are all born to die, and as scripture reminds us, death will come like a thief in the night.

WAVES

HOW THEN CAN we understand the waves of "life and joy" and the conflicting waves of "death and suffering"?

Recently I witnessed a simple example of love becoming manifest in one of the Marches towns that have grown up over the centuries on the borders between England and Wales. It was a Saturday morning in February. I had become aware that leaning against an ancient, rustic brick wall, camouflaged by many years of grime and dirty grease, was an old man; the remnants of his once expensive camel-haired overcoat gave an air of homelessness.

I heard a sweet voice, 'Here you are Jim'.

The lady and Jim exchanged a few words and then parted. And I wondered who felt most complete after such an encounter. Was Jim's suffering, and his acceptance of other people's kindness, an essential catalyst for love to develop?

Life is filled with waves of pleasure, joy, pain and suffering. To me, pleasure is a surface reaction and short-lived; joy is an inner resonance of the spirit deep within, enduring after pleasure has evaporated. Pain is also a temporary thing, it comes and it goes. Suffering endures after pain has abated. Pleasure and pain are of the body, but joy and suffering are reflections of the mind.

Pain and suffering are not easy to measure. For example, in the heat of battle limbs can be cleaved from the body with less pain than the unexpected prick from a rose thorn. Suffering is a measure of our sensitivity, a painful form of mental frustration often for being misinterpreted, or more probably reflecting our inability to come to terms with a new situation in which we find ourselves.

There is so much suffering which seems to be unhelpful and meaningless.

Why should my own son, Jonathan, have been knocked senseless and mindless only a few weeks before his final degree examinations, (thankfully he later made a full recovery).

Why should so many, suffer the crippling betrayal of child abuse?

My father, in the last thirty years of his life, was involved in a car accident, had prolonged life-threatening bronchitis, a coronary heart attack, cancer of the lip, a severe stroke, cancer of the bowels, operations for hernia, cancer of the lungs, prostrate gland removal and he finally died of gangrene. I can't spot any obvious physical advantage in that catalogue of pain! He often commented on his own suffering, but mostly his concern was not that he would die, but that he would leave my mother, "And how would she cope?" Even though he suffered much, he was quick to offer his love and concern to his family. In fact, in general, as he grew older he grew more gentle, tolerant and understanding.

The Dalai Lama, in his book *The Buddhism of Tibet,* perhaps has the beginning of an answer to this dichotomy, "Pleasure and pain (joy and suffering) ... do not arise from superficial external factors alone; one must have their internal causes. These are the potencies or latencies of the mind. These potencies are in a dormant state; they are activated when one encounters external causes".

There is no doubt that the natural world is reflected within our minds and that God's universe has an interplay of "darkness and light", echoed in a more sexual way by ancient Chinese tradition of the interlocking shapes of the dark, receptive, feminine *yin* and the bright, assertive, masculine *yang*. However, I have often asked myself, "Why didn't an all powerful God create a painless world?" The suffering of individuals is hard to fathom. But, in the end, just like that Old Testament character, Job, I stopped questioning God about why we should suffer. Or about why other people seem to suffer more than I do, for I cannot truly know the suffering or the joy of another.

The thorns of life could simply be a way that our creator reminds us of danger. Pain has survival value and prompts us to remove our hands when in contact with fire; which makes me realize just how unfortunate are those individuals who cannot feel pain and are extremely vulnerable. Could it be that the suffering and sadness we feel somehow enhances our very soul, a form of preparation, or building up exercise, for what is to come? As physical pain guides us to look after our physical well-being, so suffering could be a personal wake-up call guiding us to become aware of that part of us which is transcendental, the enduring *me*, and to appreciate more our very *being*.

It seems that to make heartfelt love manifest, suffering is required. The Biblical parable of the Good Samaritan, who helped a stranger, needed that stranger to be beaten nearly to death for active compassion to be realized.

Have we been confusing the waves of joy and suffering in our lives with the sea of life itself? Could it be that the good things and bad things that happen to us in our lives are like the surface waves of a great ocean? To judge the meaning of each wave of the ocean of life detracts from seeking the depths, and we ignore the meaning of the holistic whole. It is the breaking waves on the shore of life that fool us into believing that they are the mighty ocean itself.

Perhaps it is only the development of love that matters in the end. For example, the abolition of slavery came about chiefly through Christian movements, which gathered pace from George Fox's Society of Friends (Quakers), and his "valiant sixty" evangelists. It became the seed of the evangelical movements of the eighteenth and nineteenth centuries. It was the practice of the Christian doctrine of love that finally turned the tide, by making slavery a moral, not an economic issue. And much of Western social care stems from Christian practice over the centuries; although the spirit, the Holy Spirit, which ignited the visions in humanity has, for many, been long forgotten.

I find it strange, even sad, that the good gifts of God all too often bring about selfishness, greed, and over-indulgence in our base desires, while the pain and suffering of others can bring about the blossoming of compassionate love. While human calamity will bring people flocking to a place of worship, the strong and prosperous can soon forget God.

I pray that those carrying the burden of intelligence or wealth do not wait until it is too late before they realize that their worldly advantages are but mirages, so very temporary.

I believe that life is not about questioning why suffering exists, but about helping to alleviate it. It is not about questioning why poverty exists, but how to remove it. It is not about questioning why the "four selfish horses" exist within each of our minds, but how to tame them.

In truth every act of charity, every thought of sympathy, every action of help, and every good deed develops a deeper, peaceful joy of the soul. It is this *renewal* of the soul, which allows us to smile benevolently at all the world has to offer. For some, inner strength develops to such an extent that they can even show love and concern for their persecutors, no matter how severe the pain! While enduring the agony of the cross, Jesus still managed to ask God to think kindly of his killers, "Forgive them for they know not what they do".

I remember with great affection the joyful days of my childhood seaside holidays; the freedom of the beach, the yielding sand and the laughing waters. Once there was disaster in my little scampering world when something sharp caused blood to spurt uncontrollably from my foot. I was suddenly aware of being lost on a great beach filled with unknown people. But my caring parent was there, all the time, and arrived at my side as soon as I called out.

A caring parent reminds me of God, waiting nearby in case we call out. God is there for us when we are in crises. God is present all the time. So often it seems that it is through crises that God is found. When all is well we do not notice the love of our creator.

GOD'S UNIVERSE

WE HAVE TRAVELED from stardust into many lands; to dream new dreams of cooperation - not conflict; intelligence - not blindness; motivation and synchronicity - not chance alone; to brush against science, uniqueness and our interconnected universe; to set our consciousness against the eternal puzzle of Self and *being*; to wander into everyday joys and suffering, and to dip our toes into meditation and prayer.

God is the Divine Intelligence within, and yet beyond all these things. On times we become aware that the vibrations of our very souls are being energized, stroked by that master cello player, bringing to us harmonic vibrations of sheer joy. It is then that we recognize that life is a gift of beauty, happiness and pleasure. God has presented us with so many possibilities: to play like dolphins in the sea of life; to sit motionlessly meditating and praying; to accumulate wealth and power; to achieve international recognition. The list is endless.

There is suffering and death all around us. To reveal the meaning of such agony and conflict we have to pause, take a deep breath, and just *be*. Then, in God's good time, we may find wisdom and grace through contemplation and meditative prayers.

We develop, moment by moment, thought by thought, decision by decision, action by action as the days, months and years roll by, until finally the dawn breaks and we see that our gift of life is but an opportunity to shape our destiny, and to become that which God desires. It is in being kind, open and loving to others that we truly develop. It is in our doing, that we become part of God's plan, and slowly an understanding of the permanence of our existence unfolds.

How can one understand joy, if there is no sorrow? Succinctly put by well-known Crickhowell artist, Janet Reed, who once said to me, "It is the surrounding space that truly shows up the object".

Some only see life as a maze either to endure or to own, while others see life as a place where God's purpose is developed. What then is God's universe actually for? What is the true purpose of the universe of good and evil? The totality has been for me extremely difficult to visualize, then one day, during a meditative prayer, the following analogy proved to be very helpful to me. It uses the idea of the "good seed" as a metaphor for individuals who strive to mimic God's work:

The universe is like a huge container which holds good and evil, meaning and non-meaning, randomness and synchronicity, joy and suffering. And yet within there are divine sparks like seeds immersed in a sea of black and white, aggression and love. The seed's husk is like that protective membrane around the first true life form; only instead of two types of molecules it is a composite of evil and love. The outer part of the membranes is that which we call evil - all that causes suffering, the four wild horses of the mind, the greed, the selfishness. It faces the totality of the physical universe with all its turmoil. The inner part of the little seed's membrane is pure altruistic compassion that holds consciousness like a magnetic field can hold 'white hot flux of molten plasma'. The good seed contains grace-filled consciousness that refines pure love, unbounded love; repaying evil with love, hate with love, and all things with love. It asks for no reward, seeks no prize, it is pure and unblemished. It is rare and precious.

God's universe demands that although we may disagree with other people's way of life, we learn to live in harmony, seeing all our differences as a joy. Then a synergy will occur, and evolution will take one more giant step. The next level of complexity will become manifest.

The result will be something unimaginable, beyond our individuality. It will be like when the hundred, million, million individual cells of our body became one whole. Each one protected by the others, yet each one willing to sacrifice self, for the sake of the whole.

For Christians this new evolved reality has been predicted for over two thousand years. It is the coming of the Kingdom of God. It seems to me that this, with God's Grace, will become manifest when we all follow such scriptural advice as, "Finally, be united, all of you in thought and feeling; be full of brotherly affection, kindly and humble. Do not repay wrong with wrong, or abuse with abuse; on the contrary, respond with blessing, for a blessing is what God intends you to receive" (*1 Peter* 3:8,9).

THE RAINBOW

ON A WALK across the riverside fields of Pontcanna in Cardiff I recollect being unexpectedly overawed. For some reason I had stopped walking and in bending down, perceived another world. At my feet the autumn grass supported myriads of glittering silver, spider threads; a shimmering carpet, a fantasy world that stretched to the setting sun; sparkling jewels of nature.

As well as the natural sights with their staggering awesomeness, there is the beauty of sounds; from harmonious chants and song-words of religious worship to the laughing gurgles of a newborn child. Even entertaining parables can move our thinking and emotion to a higher understanding. For example I remember a, somewhat harsh, Eastern story told to me in a colorful way by Geshe-La from the Lam Rim Buddhist Centre near Raglan, Wales:

> A "hungry ghost" called to see a perfect, altruistic gentleman, a Bodhisattva king, and asked for something to eat. Yes, said the king, you may have anything you wish. But the hungry ghost asked that he might eat the king's flesh and drink his blood. All right said the king, for he was a true Bodhisattva. The hungry ghost tore at the king's flesh and ate it and looked at

the king expecting rebuff, but no, the king simply smiled. Then the hungry ghost grabbed the king's arm and plunging his teeth deep into the flesh began to suck the king's blood. Still the king did not object for a Bodhisattva gives his life to satisfy another. Finally the ghost began to reflect and change … "

Although this story sent a shudder through me, not least because I am a vegetarian, its point is very clear – it is the love that takes away others pain, sacrificial love, that fundamentally changes hearts and minds so necessary to create a truly compassionate world. Perhaps expressed in a more understandable way by that great seventeenth-century Sikh, Guru Gobind Singh ji, "Grant me this boon, O Lord, that I may never be deterred form doing good deeds."

It is from the rainbow of contrasts that much of our understanding of life is distilled. Contrasts sharpen our minds until, in utter silence, we finally comprehend God's purpose and see our destiny laid bare before us. In this book I have tried to address the contrasts of individuality and oneness, cause and effect, life and death, goodness and evil, pain and pleasure, scientific and spiritual knowledge. Of all the contrasts, perhaps the most profound is between the glorious, captivating, vibrant love, which is of this world, and an awesome, trembling, transcendental, joy-filled spiritual love for our Personal Creator, God.

The best way to illustrate what I mean is to share with you two of the most life-changing experiences that I have ever encountered, both of which involve love. They contrast, yet complement each other in many ways. The first is profound earthly love while the second is – well, perhaps it would be better for you read the second one and decide for yourself just what true love for God is all about.

On the one hand a moment of most profound worldly joy occurred many decades ago, its memory forever fresh in my mind. All my life, it seemed, I had felt a longing to share a oneness with another, and then just for one trembling moment, my world stood still in an unfathomable perfection of body, mind and spirit. I was in a place of exquisite loveliness. I was young and vibrant, lying in the lush, day-warmed grass of mid-summer, looking at clear blue skies and seeing the chattering, dancing leaves high in the poplar trees shaking with scintillating pleasure at the gentle summer breeze. Above all, I was spellbound by the closeness of the young love of my life, a love sparked firstly by physical attraction, a love enhanced by an overwhelming inner synchronistic resonance, a love now in full blossom through the rarest of human friendship. I was with the girl destiny declared I was to share the rest of my life.

On the other hand, if you want to know the true meaning of life, strip away all the greenery, strip away the cool lush grass, leave the worldly love of your life behind, take away your freedom to move and see the giant trees bare, not with the dormant bareness of winter but with the bareness of death. And if you truly want to know the ultimate reason for your gift of life imagine stopping for a while at the foot of a dead tree about 2,000 years ago, where Jesus hung. For it is there, in abject suffering of another, that we will surely begin to understand God's purpose.

But do you really want to know?

Well, if you do, let your mind dwell on the fullness of that scene.

Wait, quietly, wait expectantly.

Wait and feel as the gentle warm breezes change to the searing heat of the midday desert sun, feel your bare flesh burn with that stinging, scorching heat.

Wait and listen to the murmuring crowd, punctuated with foul shouts of ignorant glee and hear the great hush as Jesus rasps out his lasts words.

Wait and smell the death-stink of human misery while bodies excrete the stench of sweat, blood and all imaginable human fluids and solids. Wait and become overwhelmed by the distorted muscles and punctured bone of the innocent, suffering, agonized body of that Arab-Jew from Nazareth.

Wait and feel the waves of humiliation and pain sweeping through Jesus' mind as it struggles against the horror of being suffocated out of that pain- wracked, dying body.

Wait and feel the frustration of being misunderstood, the humility of being wrongly accused, the pain of being ignored and ridiculed for only offering love for that spark of divinity which is each person's soul, suffering because you have been given the knowledge that neither your torturers, nor those who do not stop their headlong dash through life, understand God's purpose.

Wait.

Wait.

For it is only in waiting and listening with a Grace-filled mind, focused through meditative prayer, and with the realization of our very *being*, that we will know why Jesus, the man, gave his all for his love of God, "Then the world will know that you sent me, and that you loved them as you loved me." *(John* 17:23(b)).

In Jesus we have a man who so loves his creator, God, is so

immersed in his need to express that love that he submits himself to one of the most painfully agonizing deaths that man has inflicted upon man. To knowingly and willingly do such a thing, not in the heat of battle, not to impress or even to show his love for mankind, but in open painful human faith, to struggle with all his being to do his Father's (God's) will, and in so doing help us to realize the great opportunity that the giver of our personal life has given to us.

The death of Jesus is not just an illustrative story as was the "hungry ghost" a little while ago. No, it was the real action of a real man that says so much about the reason for our lives, and tells me that we are not after all just mindless grains of sand, rocking back and forth at the bottom of a restless sea, making pointless marks in a world of sedimentary mud. We are in fact unique conscious individuals who have the opportunity to allow God's compassionate love to flow through us and into the world.

As we wait in humble prayerful meditation, at the foot of the Cross, the mists will clear and we will know that life is not ultimately about its own preservation, not about the comforts of the body, not about that limited fellowship that demands justice, or even mercy. No, it is about giving unconditional altruistic love to all, to take that unbelievable step of willingly giving back all the gifts of life, not grudgingly, not to appease, not frivolously, not to make others suffer guilt, not to become a martyr, not to have any reward whatsoever, not even to be enlightened, or spend eternity in "heaven". You will feel it when you stand silent, openhearted and trusting at the feet of the dying Christ figure, Jesus.

Wait there a moment with God in humble, benevolent expectation. Then you will know why you are here and realize that *true* love cannot be forced or bought, for it must by definition be *freely* given. The opportunity that God has granted each one of us in giving us life does not automatically result in love. No, true love can only be refined in the white-hot plasma of unblemished, altruistic compassion where we are moved, of our own free will, to unreservedly share our earthly gifts with others. It is in our giving that we receive a fuller understanding. Giving, that starts from the simple act of freely listening to others, who need to be listened to, and sharing in their problems – for then we give the most precious of all our gifts, the gift of our very limited time on this earth.

Even in the darkest moments we are able to choose to love, free to show love, and in so doing influence our ultimate destiny for it is based upon the love, which we are able to give to our suffering world.

From the simplest acts of giving, to the ultimate act of giving up your life with unbounded love for all, you will know your destiny as you make God's purpose manifest.

FURTHER READING

As well as selected articles in the popular press, quality periodicals and professional group publications, the following list represents some of the literature that I have found beneficial in my search for truth and meaning.

A. SCRIPTURAL

Holy Bible King James 1611 Version, Oxford University Press London: Henry Frowde

The Revised English Bible with the apocrypha, Oxford University Press; Cambridge University Press, 1989

The New Jerusalem Bible. Darton, Longman & Todd Ltd, 18th June, 1985

Holy Bible, New Revised Standard Version, Anglicised Edition, Oxford University Press 1995. ISBN 0 19 107000 9

Sri Guru Granth Sahib, translated by Manmohan Singh, Shiromani Gurdwara Parbandhak Committee Amritsar. Third Edition:

       Volume 1 Pages   1 to   150. Printed 1987

       Volume 2 Pages 151 to 346. Printed 1988

       Volume 3 Pages 347 to 536. Printed 1989

       Volume 4 Pages 537 to 727. Printed 1989

       Volume 5 Pages 728 to 875. Printed 1990

       Volume 6 Pages 876 to 1106. Printed 1991

       Volume 7 Pages 1107 to 1293. Printed 1992

       Volume 8 Pages 1294 to 1430. Printed 1992

The Holy Qur-an, King Fahd Holy Qur-an Printing Complex, according to the Royal decree number 12412, dated 27.10.1405 AH

The Upanishads, Swami Nikhilananda. Publisher Ramakrishna-Vivekananda Centre, New York
Volume 1 containing: *Katha, Isa, Kena, and Mundaka Upanishads.* Fifth edition 1990
Volume 2 containing: *Svetasvatara, Prasna, and Mandukya Upanishads, also Gaudapada's Karika.* Third Edition 1990
Volume 3 containing: *Aitareya and Bribadaranyaka Upanishads.* Third edition 1990
Volume 4 containing: *Taittiriya and Chhandogya Upanishads.* Second edition 1979

Brahma Sutra Bhasya – of Shankaracharya, Gambhirananda, Swami. Advaita Ashrama, 1983

Bhagavad-Gita (complete edition), A.C. Bhaktivedanta Swami Parbhupada. The Bhaktivedanta Book Trust. Seventh printing 1993

The Dhammapada, The sayings of the Buddha, Thomas Byrom. Shambhala Boston and London 1993

The Gospel of Sri Ramakrishna, Seventh printing 1984. Printed by Ramakrishna - Vivekananda Centre. New York, ISBN 0-911206-01-9

Bodhisattvacharyavatara, (A Guide to the Bodhisattva's Way of Life), translated by Stephen Batchelor. Sixth reprint 1993. Published by the Library of Tibetan Works and Archives. Dharamsala. ISBN 81-85102-59-7

The Gospel of Zarathustra, Duncan Greenlees. The Theosophical Pubs. House India 1951

New Testament Apocrypha – Vol 2: Writings Relating to the Apostles; Apocalypses and Related Subjects, Wilson, R McL; original text: Schneemelcher, Wilhelm. Westminster/John Knox Press. 1991, ISBN 0664218792

B SACRED

Holy Communion – Preparation and Companion. (**Walsham How, W.** 1906) Society of Promoting Christian Knowledge

Sacred Nitnem – the Devine Hymns of the Daly Prayers by the Sikhs. (**Doabia, Harbans Sing**. 1998). Sing Brothers Amritsar. ISBN 8172050968

The Authorised Daily Prayer Book of the Hebrew Congregations of the British Empire. (Translated by Rev **Singer, S**. 1912). Eyre and Spottiswoode Ltd

The Book of Common Prayer Vol 1. (1984). Church in Wales Publication

The Jap of the Name – Guru Nanak Dev's Japji Sahib. (**Singh, Narain**). All India Pingalwara Society

The Sikh Prayer Book. (**Singh, Gopal**, 1982). The World Silk Centre Inc.

The Splendour of God – Prayers and Devotions for private and corporate use. (**Croydon, Edward**. 1935). Convention Council of the Anglican Evangelical Group Movement

C GENERAL

Encyclopaedia of Religion, (2004). Macmillan Reference Books. ISBN 0028657330

Alberts, Bruce; Bray, Dennis; Lewis, Julian; Raff, Martin; Roberts, Keith; Watson, James D. *Molecular Biology of the Cell.* (2002). Garland Science. ISBN 0815316208

Andrews, Ted. *How to See and Read the Aura.* (2002). Llewellyn Publications. ISBN 0875420133

Armstrong, Karen. *Buddha.* (2004). Phoenix Paperback. ISBN 0753813408

Atwell, Robert. *Spiritual Classics from the Early Church.* (1995). National Society of Church House Publishing. ISBN 017 51 48273

Baring, Anne and Cashford, Jules. *The Myth of the Goddess.* (1991). Viking. ISBN 0670835641

Black, Deborah. *The Leaves of the Heaven Tree – The Great Compassion of the Buddha.* (1997). Dharma Publishing

Blackburn, Simon. *Ethics – a very short introduction.* (2001). Oxford University Press. ISBN 0192804421

Bloom, Steve. *In Praise of Primates.* (1999). Konemann Verlagsgesellschaft. ISBN 3829015569

Bodhi, Bhikkhu. *The Noble Eightfold Path – Way to End Suffering.* (1999). Buddhist Publication Society. ISBN 955240116X

Bohm, David. *Wholeness and the Implicate Order.* (1999). Routledge. ISBN 0415119669

Brother Lawrence. *The Practice of The Presence of God.* (1998) Samata Books India

Calder, Nigel. *Magic Universe.* (2003). Oxford University Press. ISBN 0198507925

Carter, Rita. *Mapping the Mind.* (2002) Phoenix Paperback. ISBN 0753810190

Chavda, Mahesh. *The Hidden Power of Speaking in Tongues.* (2003). Destiny Image Publishers. ISBN 0768421713

Chopra, Deepak. *Synchro Destiny.* (2003). Rider, an imprint of Ebury Press, Random House. ISBN 1844132218

Clarke Isabel . *Psychosis and Spirituality.* (2001). Whurr Publishers. ISBN 1861562020

Close, Frank; Martin, Michael; Sutton, Christine. *The Particle Odyssey.* (2002). Oxford University Press. ISBN 0198504861

Davies, Paul. *The Fifth Miracle – the search for the origin of life.* (1999). Penguin Books ISBN 0140282262

De Mello, Anthony S J. *Sadhana – a way to God.* (1997). Gujarat Sahitya Prakash.

Dunne, J. W. *An Experiment with Time.* (1939). Faber and Faber Ltd 6th Edition

Dyer, Wayne W. *Manifest Your Destiny.* (2003). Harper Collins. ISBN 0007160461

Eddy, Mary Baker. *Science and Health – with Key to the Scriptures.* (1994 first published 1875). Massachusetts Metaphysical College Boston. ISBN 0879520388

Edelman, Gerald M. *Wider than the Sky- the Phenomenal Gift of Consciousness.* (2004). Penguin Group. ISBN 0713997338

Elliot, Elizabeth. *A Path Through Suffering – discovering the relationship between God's mercy and our pain.* (1991). Servant Publications. ISBN 1856840026

Fortey, Richard. *Trilobite! – Eyewitness to Evolution.* (2000). Flamingo. ISBN 0006551386

Fortey, Richard. *The Earth – an Intimate History.* (2004). Harper Collins. 0002570114

Fortune, Dion. *The Mystical Qabalah.* (1976). Ernest Benn Ltd. ISBN 0510410014

Foster, Russell and Kreitzman, Leon. *Rhythms of Life – the Biological Clocks that Control the Daily Lives of Every Living Thing.* (2004). Profile Books. ISBN 1861972350

Galanter, Mark. *Cults – Faith, Healing, and Coercion.* (1999) Oxford University Press. ISBN 0195123700

Gale, Richard M. *On the Nature and Existence of God.* (1999). Cambridge University Press. ISBN 0521457238

Gert, Bernard. *Morality – Its Nature and Justification.* (1998). Oxford University Press. ISBN 0195122569

Grayling, A C. *The Mystery of Things.* (2004). Weidenfeld and Nicolson. ISBN 0297645595

Gribbin, John. *The Birth of Time.* (1999). Weidenfeld and Nicolson. ISBN 029782001X

Hanson, Anthony. (ed). *Teilhard Reassessed.* Darton, Longman & Todd 1970 ISBN 0 232 51108 X – Chapter 4 *The Place of Evil on a World of Evolution* by R B Smith

Haught, John F. *God After Darwin: A Theology of Evolution.* (2001). Westview Press; O Edition. ISBN 0813338786

Hawking, Stephen. *The Universe in a Nutshell.* (2001). Bantam Press. ISBN 0593048156

Hellier, Graham. *The Thoughtful Guide to Christianity.* (2003). O Books. ISBN 1903816343

Helm, Paul. *Faith and Reason.* (1999) Oxford University Press. ISBN 0192892908

Jaworski, Joseph. *Synchronicity – the Inner Path of Leadership.* (1998). Berrett-Koehler Publishers. ISBN 1576750310

John Paul II. *The Spirit Giver of Life and Love – A Catechesis on the Creed* Pauline Books and Media ISBN 0 8198 6987-2

Johnson, Steven. *Emergence.* (2001). Allen Lane The Penguin Press. ISBN 071399402

Jung, Gustav Carl. *Modern Man in Search of a soul.* (2001 first published 1933). Routledge Classics. ISBN 041525390X.

Dr Kahn, Muhammad Muhsin *The Translation of the meanings of Shih Al-Burkhart – Arabic-English Vol 1.* (1977). Hazi Publications

Kauffman, Stuart. *At Home in the Universe.* (1995). Oxford University Press. ISBN 0670847356

Kavanaugh, Kieran and Rodriguez, Otilio. *The Collected Works of St. John of the Cross.* (1979). ICS Publications. ISBN 0960087656

Krebs, Charles. J *Ecology (fifth edition) Experimental Analysis of Distribution and Abundance.* (2001). Benjamin Cummings an imprint of Addison Wesley. ISBN 0-321-04289-1

Lane, Nick. *Oxygen – The Molecule that made the World.* (2003). Oxford University Press. ISBN0198607830

Lewis, C S. *The Four Loves.* ((2002 first published 1960). Harper Collins. ISBN 0006280897

Lewis, C S. *The Problem of Pain.* (2002 first published 1940). Harper Collins. ISBN 0006280935

Lewontin, Richard. *It Ain't Necessarily So – the Dream of the Human Genome and other Illusions.* (2000). Granta Books. ISBN 1862072035

Maclaine, Shirley. *Going Within.* (1994). Bantam Press. ISBN 0553400487

MacNutt, Francis. *Healing.* ((1989). Hodder and Stoughton. ISBN 0340510358

Mann, Christopher. *Flightpaths of the Gods.* (1997). Broadcasting Support Services. ISBN 1861200250

Margulis, Lynn. *The Symbiotic Planet – a new look at evolution* (1988) Weidenfeld & Nicolson ISBN 0-297-81740-X

Martin, R P. *Carmen Christi – Philippians ii. 5-11 – in Recent Interpretation and in the Setting of Early Christian Worship.* (1967). Cambridge University Press.

Metcalfe, John. *The Beatitudes.* (1993). John Metcalfe Publishing Trust. ISBN 1870039459

Meredith Michael. *Beyond all Reasonable Doubt* (2002). OBooks ISBN 0 903816 13 0

Morgan, Elaine. *The Aquatic Ape Hypothesis.* (1999). Souvenir Press. ISBN 0285035182

Morgan, Michael. *The Space Between our Ears.* (2003). Weidenfeld and Nicolson. ISBN 029782970X

Nathan, N M L. *Will and Word – a Study in metaphysics.* (1992). Clarendon Press. ISBN 0198239548

Pinker, Steven. *The Blank Slate.* (2002). Penguin Books. ISBN 014027605X

Prabhavananda, Swami. *The Sermon on the Mount.* (1992). Vedanta Press. ISBN 0874810507

Purchas, Patience. *Faith, Hope and Love.* (1989). Jarrold Colour Publications. ISBN 0711704171

Ramsey, Michael. *Be Still and Know.* (1990). Fount Paperbacks. ISBN 000626350X

Ridley, Mark. *Evolution*. (1997). Oxford University Press. ISBN 019289878

Russell, Peter J. *Genetics*. (1996). Harper Collins. ISBN 0673523594

Ruthven, Malise. *Fundamentalism – The Search for Meaning*. (2004). Oxford University Press. ISBN 0192840916

Screech, M A. *Michael De Montaigne – four essays*. (1995) Penguin Books. ISBN 0146000374

Shannon, Father William H. *Seeking the Face of God*. (1988). Fount. ISBN 0006273785

Shaw, John C. *The Brain's Rhythms and the Mind*. (2003). Elsevier Science B V. ISBN 0444513973

Singh, Ranbir. *The Sikh Way of Life*. (1989). Central Gurmat Parchar Board.

Stapleton, Ruth Carter. *The experience of Inner Healing*. ((1978). Hodder and Stoughton. ISBN 0340228032

Steiner, George. *Heidegger*. (1982) Fontana Paperbacks. ISBN 0006333249

Taylor, John. C, *The Christ-like God*, (1992) SCM Press ISBN 0334 00179X

Tudge, Colin. *The Variety of Life – A Survey and a Celebration of All the Creatures that have ever lived*. (2000). Oxford University Press. ISBN 0198604262

Walsh, Michael. *Roots of Christianity*. (1986). Grafton Books. ISBN 0246127570

Watkins, John. *Hearing Voices – a Common Human Experience*. (1998). Hill of Content Publishing. ISBN 0855722886

Wiles, Maurice F. *God's Action in the World*. Bampton Lectures (1986) SCM Press ISBN 0-334-62028-X

Williams, Dr Rowan. *Silence and Honey Cakes- the wisdom of the desert*. (2003). Lion Publishing plc. ISBN 0 7495 5138 4

Yancey, Philip. *The Jesus I Never Knew*. (1995). Marshall Pickering. ISBN 0551029609

Young-Eisendrath, Polly and Miller, Melvin E. *The Psychology of Mature Spirituality.* (2000). Routledge. ISBN 0415179602